Everyday Life with The Father Devotional
Apostle Eric D. Harris

1

Foreword

It is amazing how far many have strayed from our original, created design. We were made by God to have an intimate relationship and fellowship with Him. Unfortunately, many have lost that connection—the beat of the heart, the awareness of a loving Father who desires to spend time with us. Their hearing has become dull due to distance, and the absence of God's voice is felt deeply, even though it is desperately needed.

We need a roadmap that leads us back to a place of communion with Him. It will show us the way back into intimacy with God, back to a place where we can reconnect with what we have lost.

With that being said, I thank God for Apostle Harris, because in his quiet time with the Lord, God has given him a key—a devotional that will provide us with an understanding and create a clear path to reconnect with our loving Father. This will allow us to experience the depth, the breadth, the width, and the height of all that God has for us.

I encourage you to read this writing. Apostle Harris has done an incredible job of guiding us along a path that will lead us to a healthier, more vibrant, rich, and impactful relationship with God. I believe he has uncovered something vital that has been missing in our pursuit of God.

Bishop Victor Hill

Senior Leader Providence Christian

Foreword

Eric Harris is a brother in Christ, a fellow minister of the Gospel, a prayer partner and a good friend. I have confidence in his walk with God and his ability to hear God's voice. When Eric shares his thoughts, it comes from a place of communion with God and His Word. His writings will enlighten you, encourage you and inspire you. If your load is heavy or you just need an uplift today, pay attention and get ready to be blessed by these devotional thoughts.

Pastor Randy Williams

Former pastor

Parkway Christian Fellowship

Birmingham Al

Foreword

"Everybody can be great, because everybody can serve. You don't have to have a college degree to serve. You don't have to make your subject and your verb agree to serve. You only need a heart full of grace, a soul generated by love." – Martin Luther King Jr.

In the depths of human aspiration, a profound paradox lies in wait. We yearn for greatness, to leave an indelible mark on the world, and to be remembered for our achievements. Yet, in our pursuit of greatness, we often overlook the fundamental key to unlocking our true potential: servanthood. It is a paradox that has puzzled philosophers and theologians for centuries, but one that holds the power to transform our lives and our relationships.

At its core, servanthood is the embodiment of the mysterium tremendum, the awe-inspiring mystery that lies at the heart of our existence. It is the manifestation of the Imago Dei, the image of God, that resides within us, calling us to serve and to love. Servanthood is not a distant ideal, but a lived reality that permeates every aspect of our daily lives. It is the humble boundary that keeps our ambition in check, reminding us that true greatness is not about self-aggrandizement, but about the selfless act of serving others.

Each of us is called and challenged to embrace the incarnation of the Kenotic Christ - the self-emptying Son of God, who, though being in the image of God, emptied Himself to become like a man in order to serve mankind.

"Who, being in very nature God, did not consider equality with God something to be used to his own advantage; rather, he made himself nothing by taking on the very nature of a servant, being made in human likeness. And being found in appearance as a man, he humbled himself by becoming obedient to death — even death on a cross!"
Philippians 2:6-8 NIV.

Servanthood, in its truest sense, is to daily receive our personal kenosis and be conformed into the image of Christ, who lived, died, and rose as a servant. And, risen, He yet lives to make intercession for us - a profound type of servanthood.

To serve is to crucify our self-interest, to lay down our own desires and ambitions for the sake of others. It is a daily reevaluation of our beliefs and conscience, a constant introspection that positions us as servants of God and of one another. Under the guidance of the Holy Spirit, Pastor Harris has crafted a devotional that invites us to embark on this journey of self-discovery and servanthood.

Through the pages of this devotional, we are reminded that servanthood is not just a lofty ideal, but a tangible reality that unfolds in the everyday moments of our lives. A hug, a kind word, a gesture of friendship, or a simple act of kindness – these are the language of servanthood, the inaudible words that speak volumes about our character and our commitment to serving others. They are the decisions we make to align ourselves with the image of Christ, our highest calling and our truest aspiration.

As we delve into the reflections and insights of this devotional, may we be compelled to reexamine our priorities and our values. May we come to understand that servanthood is not a means to an end, but an end in itself – the very elevator that lifts us to human greatness. And may we, like Pastor Harris, be inspired to live a life of servanthood, one that embodies the divine love that resides within us, and that speaks the language of kindness, compassion, and selflessness to a world in need. A daily crucifixion well worth it.

Created to serve,
Bishop L. Spenser Smith
Senior Pastor, Impact Nation
Tuscaloosa, Alabama.   2025 A.D.
January

In Loving Memory

In loving memory of my grandmother, Eloise Gilder—the sweetest, wisest, and most loving grandmother of all time. Your unwavering love and devotion to God have been a source of inspiration throughout my life. The example you set in faithfully serving Him remains a shining light, guiding me as I continue to follow Christ.

I am forever grateful for your encouragement to stay close to God and serve Him all my days. Rest in heaven, Grandma. Your legacy lives on in my heart.

Dedication

I dedicate this book first and foremost to my incredible wife, Miranda, who is truly a gift from God. I am grateful that, in His infinite wisdom, He brought us together. Thank you for your love, support, and encouragement. I love you with all my heart.

To my daughters, Jasmine, Erika, and Christian: I still marvel at why God entrusted me with the privilege of fathering three amazing girls, but I'm so glad He did. Each of you has demonstrated a deep love for God and family, and I'm so proud of you. Thank you for your unwavering love and support.

To my son-in-law, Christopher Warren, the son God gave me through marriage: I truly appreciate your hard work, dedication to family, and passion for pursuing God.

To my grandchildren—Karter, Kaidence, Avery, Jordan, and Jaden—you all hold a special place in my heart. I love each of you dearly.

To the Agape Worship Ministries family: thank you for allowing me to serve you and for consistently showing up, engaging, and striving to change the world. Your faithfulness inspires me.

Lastly, I dedicate this book to every reader. My prayer is that it serves as a tool to help you deepen your relationship with the Father and grow in your faith.

Acknowledgements

I humbly recognize that our God has created us to be interdependent, and any success I may achieve is directly tied to Him. I want to first acknowledge God, who is the source of all wisdom and strength.

Of course, as I've already recognized my incredible wife, Miranda, I must also thank her for her unwavering encouragement and insight—often given without her even realizing it.

To Minister Demita Woolfolk-Walton, the best personal assistant ever: your knowledge, skills, and ability to navigate every task have been invaluable. Your guidance through this process and your brilliance as an editor have been nothing short of remarkable. Thank you for your love, support, and dedication.

To the Tuesday morning breakfast table—Bishop Victor Hill, Pastor Lorenza Huggins, Pastor Earl Dixon, and Pastor Gary Cooper—thank you for sharpening me as we sharpen one another. The wisdom and insights shared at that table have profoundly influenced my weekly study of the Word.

Finally, to Agape Worship Ministries: you have been a constant source of inspiration for creating this content over the years. My heart's desire and goal remain to help each of you become the very best version of the believer God created you to be.

Thank you all for your love, support, and partnership in this journey.

In my daily prayer, I was prompted to reflect on two questions that surfaced during my time with the Lord: *"How can I serve God today?" and "How can I serve my wife today?"* After writing them down, I sensed the Lord impressing upon me that these questions should be a daily priority for every believer. As I continued to process what God was speaking to me, I felt Him saying that embracing these questions daily will help us grow stronger and deeper in our relationship with Him.

This divine prompting serves as a reminder:

take full advantage of the glory of God that can be revealed through your   "Everyday life with the Father".

This devotional is designed to foster intimacy with the Father. It begins with the expectation that God will speak to you during this time. Each day's entry includes:

1.   *Moments of Impartation* – Words of inspiration and revelation from the Lord to guide you.

2.   *Reflection Questions* – Designed to provoke thought, transformation, and intentionality in your walk with God.

3.   *Action Questions* – Meant to inspire you to actively serve God and others each day.

This structure is a tool to deepen your connection with God and prompt a lifestyle of intentional intimacy and service. Let these moments with the Father shape your life and bring glory to His name daily.

How to Use This Devotional

Each day begins with the same question to spark expectation that God will speak to you during your devotional time. This devotional is intentionally undated, allowing you to start at any time without feeling discouraged if you miss a day.

Titled *"Everyday life with the Father"*, this devotional is designed not only to help you grow in your relationship with Christ but also to assist you in navigating the daily challenges of life. Each day includes a prayer, a reflection question, and an action question based on the day's content, all aimed at helping you apply God's Word to your life in practical ways.

If you approach this devotional with intention and consistency, your life will be enriched by spending daily time with the Father.

TABLE OF CONTENTS

Good morning Holy Spirit, will you speak to me today.

Greater is He Who is in You

1 John 4:4

"Greater is He who is in you than He who is in the world."

#1 He is in You

As a believer, the Spirit of God resides within you. You are not alone in your struggles, decisions, or victories. The same God who created the heavens and the earth has made His dwelling in you. This truth transforms your identity—you are not merely human; you are a vessel of divine power and purpose. When you feel weak, remember that His strength is in you, and His presence is your constant source of hope and guidance.

#2 Greatness Is in You

Because He is in you, greatness resides in you. This greatness isn't about fame or accolades; it's about the power and purpose of God working through your life. You carry the DNA of the King of kings. Every gift, every talent, and every calling is imbued with divine potential. Walk with confidence, knowing you are chosen to reflect God's glory in the world. Declare today: "I am equipped, empowered, and unstoppable because His greatness is in me!"

#3 You're Greater Than What You're Facing

The challenges you face may seem overwhelming, but they are not greater than the God within you. Trials, opposition, and hardships are opportunities for God's power to shine through your life. Don't allow fear or doubt to take hold—stand firm in the truth that you are more than a conqueror through Him who loves you. Speak to your mountains and remind them: "Greater is He who is in me!"

Prayer

Lord, thank You for the reminder that You are in me and that Your greatness dwells within me. Help me to live boldly and victoriously, knowing I am equipped to overcome every obstacle. Strengthen me to face each day with confidence, knowing You are greater than anything I will encounter. In Jesus' name, Amen.

Reflection Question

What challenges are you facing today that you need to remind, "Greater is He who is in me"?

Action Question

How can I serve God today?

_____

_____

_____

_____

Good morning Holy Spirit, will you speak to me today.

Devotional: We Got It

2 Peter 1:3

"According as His divine power hath given unto us all things that pertain unto life and godliness, through the knowledge of Him that hath called us to glory and virtue."

#1 We Got It—By God's Divine Authority

God's power is the ultimate authority in heaven and earth. It is through His divine authority that He has granted us everything we need. This is not based on our works, status, or qualifications but on His sovereign will and unchanging character. When God speaks, it is done. When He gives, it is complete. Trust in the authority of God, knowing that He has equipped you to live victoriously. You lack nothing because He has already provided everything!

#2 We Got It—All Things Needed for Living and Godliness

God has left nothing out. Everything you need to navigate life—peace, provision, direction, wisdom—is already yours. Likewise, He has given you all the resources needed to grow in godliness: His Spirit, His Word, and His promises. Whether you are facing challenges in your personal life or striving to reflect His character in a broken world, His divine supply is sufficient. You don't have to earn it; it's a gift!

#3 We Got It—By Knowing God

The key to accessing all these blessings is knowing Him. It's not about casual acquaintance but a deep, growing relationship with the Lord. The more you know Him, the more you experience His divine power in your life. Through prayer, worship, and time in His Word, your understanding of His provision and promises grows, and you learn to walk confidently in what He has already given you.

Prayer

Lord, thank You for Your divine power that has given me everything I need for life and godliness. Help me to trust in Your authority, recognize the fullness of Your provision, and deepen my relationship with You. Teach me to walk in the fullness of what You have already given and reflect Your glory and virtue in my life. In Jesus' name, Amen.

Reflection Question

How can you deepen your knowledge of God today to fully access all He has given you for life and godliness?

Action Question

How can I serve God today?

_____

_____

_____

_____

Good morning Holy Spirit, will you speak to me today.

Devotional: It's Not Over

Lamentations 3:22–23 (KJV)

"It is of the LORD's mercies that we are not consumed, because his compassions fail not. They are new every morning: great is thy faithfulness."

#1 It's Not Over Because of God's Kindness (Mercies)

God's mercy is the reason we are still standing. His kindness shields us from what we deserve and offers us grace to start anew. Even when we feel overwhelmed or defeated, His mercies renew our hope. Every morning, He gives us a fresh start, a new chance to walk in His purpose. No matter how far you've strayed or how heavy the burden, remember: His mercy says, "It's not over!"

#2 It's Not Over Because of God's Love (Compassion)

God's compassion is His steadfast, unfailing love. It's a love that sees us in our brokenness and meets us with healing. It's a love that never fails, even when we do. His compassion reminds us that no mistake, no failure, and no circumstance can separate us from His care. When life feels like too much, God's love whispers, "Keep going; I am with you."

#3 It's Not Over Because of God's Faithfulness

God is faithful to His promises. His faithfulness ensures that no matter how dark or uncertain life may seem, He will see us through. He never changes, never falters, and never leaves. When you feel like giving up, remember His faithfulness. He will complete the good work He began in you. Because of His unwavering faithfulness, you can declare with confidence: "It's not over!"

Prayer

Lord, thank You for Your kindness, love, and faithfulness that remind me it's not over. When I feel weak, help me to trust in Your mercies that are new every morning. Teach me to rest in Your compassion and to rely on Your unchanging faithfulness. I give You my fears and failures, knowing You will finish what You started in my life. In Jesus' name, Amen.

Reflection Question

Which of God's attributes—His kindness, love, or faithfulness—do you need to hold onto most today as you face your challenges?

Action Question

How can I serve God today?

_____

_____

_____

_____

Good morning Holy Spirit, will you speak to me today.

Devotional: Trust the Lord

Exodus 14:14 (KJV)

"The LORD shall fight for you, and ye shall hold your peace."

#1 Trust the Lord to Keep You

God is your protector, your refuge, and your stronghold. Even in the midst of chaos, He promises to keep you. You don't have to fear the storm because the One who holds you is greater than anything you face. When you feel vulnerable, remind yourself of His faithfulness. Trust that He is watching over you and will not let you fall. Rest in the assurance that His presence surrounds you like a shield.

#2 Trust the Lord to Fight for You

The battles you face are not yours to fight alone. God steps in as your defender and champion. He sees what you cannot and works on your behalf in ways you may never fully understand. When the enemy comes against you or circumstances seem overwhelming, resist the urge to fight in your own strength. Instead, place your confidence in the Lord. His power is unmatched, and He will bring victory in His perfect way and time.

#3 Trust the Lord to Give You Peace

God doesn't just promise to fight for you; He also promises peace. This isn't just the absence of conflict—it's the presence of His calm assurance in your heart and mind. Peace comes when you release control and trust Him completely. Let go of worry, fear, and anxiety, and hold onto His promise: "Be still, and know that I am God." He will give you peace that surpasses understanding as you place your trust in Him.

Prayer

Lord, thank You for being my keeper, my defender, and my peace. I trust You to protect me, fight for me, and calm my spirit in the midst of life's challenges. Help me to release control and place my faith in Your strength. Thank You for the victory You bring and the peace You provide.

In Jesus' name, Amen.

Reflection Question

What situation do you need to surrender to the Lord today, trusting Him to fight for you and give you peace?

Action Question

How can I serve God today?

_____

_____

_____

_____

Good morning Holy Spirit, will you speak to me today.

Devotional: The Source of True Joy

Proverbs 10:28 (KJV)

"The hope of the righteous shall be gladness: but the expectation of the wicked shall perish."

#1 Know That Your Joy Originates from God

True joy begins with God. As His righteous children, our hope is grounded in His promises and character. Unlike fleeting happiness that depends on circumstances, the joy that comes from God is steadfast and unshakable. It is rooted in His faithfulness and love. When life feels uncertain, remember that your joy originates from the One who never changes. Keep your focus on Him, and let His presence be your source of gladness.

#2 Know That Your Joy Initiates from Your Heart

Joy flows from a heart aligned with God. When your heart is filled with His Word, His Spirit, and His peace, joy naturally overflows. Guard your heart against negativity, bitterness, or doubt, and nurture it with prayer, gratitude, and worship. Your joy isn't determined by external circumstances but by the condition of your inner life. Let your heart be a wellspring of hope and gladness as you trust in God's goodness.

#3 Know That Your Joy Is Fulfilled by Your Actions

Joy is not just a feeling—it's an expression that is reflected in how we live. Your actions—whether it's serving others, sharing kindness, or walking in obedience—help bring your joy to its full potential. As you live out your faith, the hope of righteousness turns into tangible gladness, blessing both you and those around you. Choose to act in ways that reflect the joy God has placed within you.

Prayer

Lord, thank You for being the source of my joy. Help me to keep my heart aligned with You so that my life overflows with gladness. Teach me to act in ways that reflect the joy and hope You have given me. Strengthen me to live as a light, sharing Your love and joy with the world. In Jesus' name, Amen.

Reflection Question

How can you align your heart and actions today to reflect the joy that originates from God?

Action Question

How can I serve God today?

_____

_____

_____

_____

Good morning Holy Spirit, will you speak to me today.

Devotional: Strength for the Weary

Isaiah 40:29 (KJV).

"He giveth power to the faint; and to them that have no might He increaseth strength."

#1 Fatigue Is Inevitable

Life's demands can leave us physically, emotionally, and spiritually drained. Fatigue is a natural part of the human experience, but it's not the end of the story. Even the strongest among us will grow weary at times. Acknowledging your limitations is not a sign of weakness but an opportunity to lean into the limitless strength of God. When you feel like you can't take another step, remember that your exhaustion is the very place where God's power can begin to work.

#2 God Will Give You Staying Power

When you're faint and weary, God gives you the endurance to keep going. His staying power doesn't come from human effort but from His Spirit working in you. He equips you to persevere through trials and challenges, renewing your strength in moments when you feel like giving up. Trust that His grace is sufficient to carry you, no matter how long the journey or how tough the road ahead.

#3 God Will Give You Production Power

God doesn't just help you survive—He enables you to thrive. When you feel like you have no might left, He increases your strength, empowering you to accomplish what you couldn't in your own ability. Whether it's fulfilling your purpose, managing responsibilities, or impacting others, God's power enables you to be fruitful even in your weakness. Surrender your exhaustion to Him, and watch as He multiplies your efforts with His divine strength.

Prayer

Lord, thank You for giving power to the faint and increasing strength to those who have no might. I acknowledge my limitations and ask for Your staying power to help me endure and Your production power to help me thrive. Renew my strength daily as I trust in You. Thank You for being my source of power and hope. In Jesus' name, Amen.

Reflection Question

Where in your life do you need God's staying power and production power to renew your strength today?

Action Question

How can I serve God today?

_____

_____

_____

_____

Good morning Holy Spirit, will you speak to me today.

Devotional: Freedom Through Seeking God

Psalm 34:4(KJV)
"I sought the LORD, and He heard me, and delivered me from all my fears."

1.   God Wants to Hear from You

God longs for a personal relationship with you. He isn't distant or indifferent to your struggles. He invites you to call on Him, to share your fears, and to bring your burdens before Him. Seeking God is an act of trust, acknowledging that He cares deeply for you.

2.   God Will Answer You

God's ears are always open to His children. His answer may not always come in the way or timing we expect, but He promises to respond. His answers bring clarity, peace, and hope to troubled hearts.

3.   God Will Set You Free

Fear can paralyze us, but God's presence brings freedom. He delivers us from the grip of fear, replacing it with His perfect peace. His deliverance might come through His Word, through prayer, or through the encouragement of others, but it always leads to freedom.

Prayer:

Lord, I thank You that You hear me when I call out to You. Today, I bring my fears and anxieties before You, trusting in Your power to deliver me. Help me to seek You wholeheartedly and walk in the freedom You have promised. In Jesus' name, Amen.

Reflection Question:

What steps can I take to seek God more?

Action Question:

How can I serve God today?

_____

_____

_____

_____

Good morning Holy Spirit, will you speak to me today.

Devotional: The Power of Patience

James 1:4 (KJV)

"But let patience have her perfect work, that ye may be perfect and entire, wanting nothing."

#1 Be Patient

Patience is not just waiting; it is trusting God in the process. In a world that often demands instant results, patience calls us to slow down and rely on God's timing. While waiting can be difficult, it's in those moments that faith is strengthened and character is built. Trust that God's timing is perfect and that He is working behind the scenes for your good.

#2 Patience Breeds Growth

Patience allows God to do His refining work in us. When we endure trials with faith, we grow in wisdom, maturity, and resilience. Each season of waiting or challenge is an opportunity for God to shape us into the people He has called us to be. Instead of resisting the process, embrace it, knowing that patience is producing something far greater in you than you can imagine.

#3 Growth Brings Capacity

As patience develops growth, growth expands our capacity to handle more of God's blessings and purpose. When we allow God to work in us through patience, He equips us to steward the fullness of His plans. What you are enduring today is preparing you for what God has in store tomorrow. Stay faithful in the process, and trust that your capacity is being enlarged for greater things.

Prayer

Lord, help me to embrace patience as part of Your perfect work in my life. Teach me to trust in Your timing and to allow the process to produce growth and maturity in me. Expand my capacity to receive and steward all that You have planned. Strengthen me to remain faithful as You prepare me for the fullness of Your blessings. In Jesus' name, Amen.

Write two things that stand out from today's scripture

Reflection Question

How can you let patience work in your current season of waiting or challenge? What growth is God producing in you right now?

Action Question:

How can I serve God today?

Good morning Holy Spirit, will you speak to me today.

Devotional: Trust in the Everlasting Strength

Isaiah 26:4 (KJV).

"Trust ye in the LORD for ever: for in the LORD JEHOVAH is everlasting strength."

#1 It's on You (You Trust Him)

The first step to experiencing God's strength is choosing to trust Him. Trust is a deliberate act of faith—a decision to place your confidence in His ability rather than your own. Life may throw uncertainties your way, but your responsibility is clear: trust in the Lord. When you surrender your doubts and fears, you open the door for God to move powerfully in your situation.

#2 It's Always on You (Trust Him Forever)

Trusting God is not a one-time act but a lifelong commitment. The verse reminds us to trust Him forever. This means trusting Him in every season—good or bad, easy or difficult. Forever trust means relying on God's faithfulness, even when you can't see the outcome. As you develop a pattern of continuous trust, your faith grows deeper, and your relationship with Him becomes unshakable.

#3 It's Really on Him (God's Got You)

While trust is your responsibility, the weight of the situation is ultimately on God. He is the source of everlasting strength. His power doesn't run out, His faithfulness doesn't falter, and His ability to sustain you doesn't waver. When you lean on Him, you can rest in the assurance that He's got you. Whatever you're facing, know that God's strength will carry you through.

Prayer

Lord, I choose to trust You today and every day. Help me to rely on Your everlasting strength instead of my own abilities. Teach me to trust You in every season and to find peace in knowing that You've got me in Your hands. Thank You for being my source of unfailing strength and security. In Jesus' name, Amen.

Reflection Question

What area of your life do you need to surrender to God's everlasting strength and trust Him completely?

Action Question:

How can I serve God today?

_____

_____

_____

_____

Good morning Holy Spirit, will you speak to me today.

Devotional: New Mercies Every Morning

Lamentations 3:22–23 (KJV).

"It is of the LORD's mercies that we are not consumed, because his compassions fail not. They are new every morning: great is thy faithfulness."

#1 God's Love Never Fails

God's mercy and compassion are rooted in His unfailing love. No matter how difficult life may feel, His love remains constant. It is His mercy that keeps us from being consumed by life's challenges or our own shortcomings. You can trust that His love will never fail you, even in your darkest moments. Rest in the truth that His compassion is greater than any struggle you face.

#2 God's Faithfulness Never Ends

God's faithfulness is eternal and unchanging. He is steadfast in His promises and unwavering in His care for you. Unlike human faithfulness, which can falter, God's faithfulness endures forever. He has been faithful in the past, and He will be faithful today and in the days to come. His consistency is a foundation on which you can stand with confidence and hope.

#3 It's Morning

Every morning brings a fresh start. God renews His mercies with each new day, giving you the grace and strength to face whatever lies ahead. Yesterday's mistakes, pain, and burdens do not define you because God's compassion gives you a clean slate. Today is an opportunity to embrace His love, trust in His faithfulness, and walk forward in His grace. It's morning—receive His new mercies with a grateful heart.

Prayer

Lord, thank You for Your unfailing love, endless faithfulness, and new mercies that greet me each morning. Help me to trust in Your compassion and lean on Your faithfulness throughout this day. I give You my fears, failures, and burdens, knowing that Your grace is sufficient for everything I face. Thank You for being the God of new beginnings. In Jesus' name, Amen.

Reflection Question:

How can you embrace God's new mercies today and live in the confidence of His unfailing love and faithfulness?

Action Question:

How can I serve God today?

_____

_____

_____

_____

Good morning Holy Spirit, will you speak to me today.

Devotional: Strength and Peace From the Lord

Psalm 29:11 (KJV).

"The LORD will give strength unto his people; the LORD will bless his people with peace."

#1 It's the Lord for Me

In every season and circumstance, the Lord is the one we can depend on. People, situations, and even our own strength may fail, but the Lord remains constant. He is the source of everything we need. When life feels overwhelming, declare, "It's the Lord for me!" He is your foundation, your protector, and the one who sustains you. Fix your eyes on Him, for He is all you truly need.

#2 He's Strength to Me

The Lord doesn't just promise strength—He gives it. Whether you're facing trials, carrying heavy burdens, or simply feeling weary, His strength is available to you. This isn't a temporary boost; it's divine empowerment that enables you to persevere and overcome. When you feel weak, lean into His strength and let Him renew your energy and spirit. His strength is made perfect in your weakness.

#3 He's Peace to Me

God's peace isn't just the absence of conflict—it's the presence of His calm and assurance in your life. He blesses His people with a peace that surpasses all understanding, guarding your heart and mind. When chaos surrounds you, His peace reminds you that He is in control. Rest in the blessing of His peace, knowing that nothing can shake you when you are anchored in Him.

Prayer

Lord, thank You for being my strength and peace. I trust You to provide what I need for every situation I face. Help me to rely on Your strength when I am weak and to embrace Your peace when life feels uncertain. You are my everything, and I give You all the praise and glory. In Jesus' name, Amen.

Reflection Question

Where in your life do you need God's strength and peace today? How can you fully depend on Him to meet your needs?

Action Question:

How can I serve God today?

_____

_____

_____

_____

Good morning Holy Spirit, will you speak to me today.

Devotional: Choose to Draw Near

Psalm 73:28 (KJV).

"But it is good for me to draw near to God: I have put my trust in the Lord GOD, that I may declare all thy works."
—

#1 Choose the Good Part

Drawing near to God is the best choice you can make. In the busyness of life, it's easy to get distracted, but nothing compares to the peace and fulfillment found in His presence. Like Mary sitting at Jesus' feet, we must choose the good part—seeking Him above all else. Make time each day to draw close through prayer, worship, and reading His Word. When you choose to draw near, you find strength, guidance, and a deeper relationship with Him.

#2 Choose to Trust Him

Trusting God is a choice, even when circumstances seem uncertain. When you draw near to Him, you discover His faithfulness and power to sustain you. Placing your trust in Him means surrendering your fears, doubts, and plans to His perfect will. Let your faith in Him be the foundation of your life. Trusting God isn't just an act of obedience—it's the key to living in peace and confidence.

#3 Choose to Tell It

When you've experienced God's goodness, you can't keep it to yourself. Sharing His works is an act of worship and a way to encourage others. Declare His faithfulness, provision, and love so others can see His power at work in your life. Your testimony can be the spark that draws someone else closer to Him. Choose to tell others what the Lord has done, giving Him all the glory.

Prayer

Lord, help me to choose the good part by drawing near to You every day. I put my trust in You, knowing that You are faithful in all things. Give me the boldness to declare Your works and share Your goodness with others. Thank You for being my strength, my refuge, and my God. In Jesus' name, Amen.

Reflection Question

How can you draw near to God today, trust Him more deeply, and share His works with those around you?

Action Question:

How can I serve God today?

_____

_____

_____

_____

Good morning Holy Spirit, will you speak to me today.

Devotional: Expect God to Move

Micah 7:7 (KJV).

"Therefore I will look unto the LORD; I will wait for the God of my salvation: my God will hear me."

#1 Expect God to Hear You

God is not distant or inattentive. When you pray, you can have confidence that He hears you. Micah's declaration shows a heart that trusts God to listen and respond. When you bring your needs, fears, and hopes before Him, trust that your words do not fall on deaf ears. Approach Him in faith, knowing He delights in hearing from His children.

#2 Expect God to Show Up

Waiting on God requires patience, but it also requires expectation. Micah chose to wait with confidence, believing that God would act in His perfect timing. God's presence brings hope and assurance, even in difficult circumstances. Trust that He is working behind the scenes, orchestrating things for your good and His glory. Keep looking to Him, knowing He will show up right when you need Him.

#3 Expect God to Save

God is not only a God who hears and shows up—He is a God who saves. He delivers, restores, and redeems His people. Whatever you're facing, trust that God's power is more than enough to rescue you. Salvation isn't just about eternal life; it's also about His ability to save you in the here and now—whether from sin, fear, or life's challenges. Expect Him to be your Savior in every sense of the word.

Prayer

Lord, I choose to look to You and wait on You with great expectation. I trust that You hear my prayers, that You will show up in my life, and that You will save me in every situation. Help me to remain patient and confident in Your power and faithfulness. Thank You for being the God of my salvation. In Jesus' name, Amen.

Reflection Question

What are you waiting on God for today, and how can you trust Him to hear, show up, and save in your situation?

Action Question:

How can I serve God today?

_____

_____

_____

_____

Good morning Holy Spirit, will you speak to me today.

Devotional: God's Comfort in the Chaos

Psalm 94:19 (KJV).

"In the multitude of my thoughts within me thy comforts delight my soul."

#1 Doubts Are Imminent

Doubt often creeps in when life feels uncertain or overwhelming. The "multitude of thoughts" that the psalmist speaks of reminds us that doubts are part of the human experience. But even when doubt tries to take root, God's truth remains steady. He meets us in our questions and reassures us with His unchanging promises.

#2 Anxiety Is Real

Anxiety can feel like a flood of thoughts and emotions that are hard to contain. It's a battle of the mind and heart that many face daily. God acknowledges your struggles and offers His peace in the midst of your anxiety. His Word becomes an anchor, steadying you when fear tries to overwhelm.

#3 Overthinking Is a Thing

Our minds often race, replaying situations or imagining outcomes that may never happen. Overthinking can lead to exhaustion and despair. But God invites us to stop striving and to trust Him instead. When your thoughts feel like a whirlwind, pause, and let His presence calm the storm.

#4 God Is There

No matter how chaotic your thoughts may feel, God is always present. His comforts—His promises, His Spirit, and His peace—bring delight to your soul. He doesn't just calm your mind; He fills your heart with joy and hope. When your thoughts seem overwhelming, remember that God's presence is greater. He is your refuge and strength, ready to surround you with His love.

Prayer

Lord, in the midst of my doubts, anxieties, and overthinking, I thank You for being my comfort and delight. Help me to trust You when my thoughts feel overwhelming. Fill me with Your peace and remind me that You are always near. Thank You for being my steady anchor in the storms of life. In Jesus' name, Amen.

Reflection Question

How can you turn to God's comfort the next time your thoughts feel overwhelming or anxious?

Action Question:

How can I serve God today?

_____

_____

_____

_____

Good morning Holy Spirit, will you speak to me today.

Devotional: Trusting the Beauty of God's Timing

Ecclesiastes 3:11 (KJV).

"He hath made everything beautiful in his time: also he hath set the world in their heart, so that no man can find out the work that God maketh from the beginning to the end." #1 God's Timing Is What Matters

Life often tempts us to rush ahead of God or question His timing. Yet, this verse reminds us that God makes everything beautiful in His time, not ours. His timing is never late, even when it feels slow to us. Trust that He is working things out in ways you can't yet see, and rest in the assurance that His timing is always perfect.

#2 God's Peace Is in Eternity

God has set eternity in our hearts, giving us a glimpse of something greater than the present moment. This eternal perspective reminds us that the peace we seek isn't tied to temporary circumstances but to the hope of God's eternal plan. His peace surpasses understanding and points us to the promise of life with Him forever. Fix your heart on eternity, where His peace abides.

#3 God's Plans Are Perfect

While we may not fully understand what God is doing from beginning to end, we can trust that His plans are perfect. Every detail of your life is part of His divine design, woven together for His glory and your good. When life feels uncertain or incomplete, remind yourself that God's work is not finished—and it will be beautiful.

Prayer

Lord, thank You for reminding me that Your timing is perfect, Your peace is eternal, and Your plans are good. Help me to trust You in the waiting, to rest in Your eternal promises, and to see the beauty in Your unfolding work. Strengthen my faith as I surrender to Your perfect will. In Jesus' name, Amen.

Reflection Question

How can you trust God's timing and plans in areas of your life where you feel uncertain or impatient?

Action Question:

How can I serve God today?

_____

_____

_____

_____

Good morning Holy Spirit, will you speak to me today.

Devotional: God's Radiant Grace

Numbers 6:25 (KJV)

"The LORD makes his face shine upon thee, and be gracious unto thee."

#1 God Is Smiling at You

Imagine the Lord's face shining upon you—a radiant expression of His love and favor. This blessing speaks of God's delight in His people. He's not distant or disapproving; He's smiling at you with joy and affection. When you feel unseen or unworthy, remember that God looks upon you with kindness and warmth, offering you His love without condition.

#2 God's Grace Is on You

God's grace is more than a gift; it's His power and favor working in your life. His grace covers your weaknesses, forgives your sins, and empowers you to live for Him. No matter what you face, His grace is sufficient to sustain and bless you. Rest in the assurance that His unmerited favor surrounds you, enabling you to walk confidently in His light.

Prayer

Lord, thank You for shining Your face upon me and surrounding me with Your grace. Help me to live in the joy of knowing You delight in me and to rely on Your grace every step of the way. Let Your light guide me and Your favor sustain me. In Jesus' name, Amen.

Reflection Question

How can you live today with the confidence that God is smiling at you and His grace is covering you?

Action Question:

How can I serve God today?

_____

_____

_____

_____

Good morning Holy Spirit, will you speak to me today.

Devotional: God's Got Answers

Jeremiah 33:3 (KJV)

"Call unto me, and I will answer thee, and shew thee great and mighty things, which thou knowest not."

#1 Make the Call

God invites you to call on Him. Whether you're in need, confused, or simply seeking direction, He's ready to hear from you. Prayer is your direct line to the Creator of the universe. Don't hesitate—bring your questions, concerns, and dreams to Him. He promises to listen when you reach out in faith.

#2 Expect an Answer

God doesn't just listen; He responds. His answers may come in unexpected ways, but they will always be perfect and timely. Trust that when you call, God is working on your behalf. Even when you don't see immediate results, He is faithful to answer in ways that are beyond what you can imagine. Expect Him to reveal great and mighty things that only He can do.

#3 Get Excited

Anticipate God's response with joy and excitement! He promises not only to answer but to reveal extraordinary things that surpass human understanding. God's plans for you are bigger than you can dream, and His answers are filled with purpose and power. Stay expectant and ready for Him to move in amazing ways.

Prayer

Lord, thank You for being a God who hears and answers when I call. Help me to trust in Your timing and to expect Your great and mighty works in my life. Stir my heart with excitement as I wait for Your plans to unfold. Thank You for always being faithful. In Jesus' name, Amen.

Reflection Question

What can you ask God for today, trusting that He will answer and reveal something amazing in your life?

Action Question:

How can I serve God today?

_____

_____

_____

_____

Good morning Holy Spirit, will you speak to me today.

Devotional: Keep Trusting Him

Psalm 62:8 (KJV).

"Trust in him at all times; ye people, pour out your heart before him: God is a refuge for us. Selah."

#1 Trust Him Now

No matter the season or situation, God is worthy of your trust right now. Whether you're walking through joy, uncertainty, or pain, place your confidence in Him. Trust isn't reserved for when everything makes sense; it's for the moments when you need His strength the most. Make the decision to trust Him today, knowing He is in control.

#2 Trust Him With Your Heart

God invites you to pour out your heart to Him. Whether your heart is heavy with fear, broken with pain, or filled with praise, He wants it all. Trusting Him means being honest with Him, holding nothing back. Share your deepest concerns and your greatest joys, knowing He cares deeply for you.

#3 Trust the Safe Place

God is your refuge—a safe place where you can find shelter, comfort, and strength. In His presence, there is no fear, condemnation, or rejection. Trust the security of His love and protection. When life feels uncertain, run to Him. He will always be the safe place you can rely on.

Prayer

Lord, I choose to trust You at all times, in every situation. Help me to pour out my heart to You, knowing that You care for me and are my refuge. Thank You for being my safe place, my strength, and my peace. I rest in Your faithful love. In Jesus' name, Amen.

Reflection Question

What part of your heart do you need to pour out to God today, trusting Him as your refuge?

Action Question:

How can I serve God today?

_____

_____

_____

_____

Good morning Holy Spirit, will you speak to me today.

Devotional: He's Keeping Me

Numbers 6:24 (KJV)"

"The LORD bless thee, and keep thee."

#1 What a Blessing

God's blessing is more than material things—it's His presence, protection, and favor over your life. To be blessed by God is to be loved, cared for, and held in His hands. Pause and reflect on the incredible gift it is to know that the Creator of the universe is mindful of you, blessing and keeping you each day.

#2 Walk in the Blessing

Living in God's blessing means walking confidently in the knowledge that He is with you. Trust Him in every step, knowing that His guidance and provision go before you. His blessing isn't just something to admire—it's something to live out. Let His favor shape your actions, words, and relationships as you walk in His light.

#3 The Blessing Is a Keeper

God doesn't just bless you—He keeps you. His keeping is His protection and sustenance, ensuring that no matter what challenges come your way, He will hold you steady. The blessing of God is a constant source of strength, peace, and security. When you feel weak or vulnerable, remember that the Keeper of your soul is watching over you with perfect love.

Prayer

Lord, thank You for blessing me and keeping me every day. Help me to walk in Your favor, trusting Your protection and guidance. I am grateful that Your blessing is not temporary but eternal. Thank You for being the Keeper of my soul. In Jesus' name, Amen.

Reflection Question

How can you live confidently today, knowing that God is both blessing and keeping you?

Action Question:

How can I serve God today?

_____

_____

_____

_____

Good morning Holy Spirit, will you speak to me today.

Devotional: The Experience

Nahum 1:7 (KJV)

"The LORD is good, a strong hold in the day of trouble; and he knoweth them that trust in him." Experience God's Goodness

God's goodness isn't just an idea—it's something to experience in your everyday life. His kindness, love, and provision are tangible reminders of His nature. Even in hard times, His goodness surrounds you, offering hope and joy. Take a moment to reflect on how His goodness has carried you through and thank Him for His unwavering faithfulness.

Experience God's Protection

In the day of trouble, God is your stronghold. He is your protector, shielding you from harm and keeping you safe in His care. No trouble is too great for Him to handle, and no fear is beyond His reach. When the storms of life rage, you can take refuge in His strength, knowing He will never let you go.

Experience God's Hiding Place

God knows those who trust in Him and provides a hiding place for them. In His presence, there is peace, security, and rest. When the pressures of life weigh heavy, He invites you to hide in Him—to find comfort and renewal under His wings. Let His presence be your sanctuary, a safe place to regain strength and courage.

Prayer

Lord, thank You for allowing me to experience Your goodness, protection, and hiding place. You are my stronghold in the day of trouble and my peace in every storm. Help me to trust You more deeply and to rest in the assurance of Your love and care. In Jesus' name, Amen.

Reflection Question

How can you lean into God's goodness and protection during your current challenges?

Action Question:

How can I serve God today?

_____

_____

_____

_____

Good morning Holy Spirit, will you speak to me today.

Devotional: Living in God's Love

1 John 4:11 (KJV)

"Beloved, if God so loved us, we ought also to love one another."

#1 God Proved His Love

God's love is more than words—it's action. He demonstrated His love by sending Jesus to die for our sins. This ultimate sacrifice is proof of how deeply and unconditionally God loves us. Reflect on this truth: you are loved completely, not because of what you've done but because of who God is. Let this reminder fill your heart with gratitude and confidence.

#2 We Must Show His Love

If God has loved us so greatly, we are called to extend that love to others. Loving one another is not optional; it's evidence of God's work in our lives. Whether through forgiveness, kindness, or compassion, showing His love reflects His nature to the world. Make it your mission to be a living example of His love, especially to those who need it most.

Prayer

Lord, thank You for proving Your love through the gift of Jesus Christ. Help me to receive Your love fully and to show it to others in my actions and words. Teach me to love as You have loved me, so that others may see You through me. In Jesus' name, Amen.

Write two things that stand out from today's scripture?

Reflection Question

Who can you intentionally show God's love to today, and
how will you do it?

Action Question:

How can I serve God today?

_____

_____

_____

_____

Good morning Holy Spirit, will you speak to me today.

Devotional: Keep Pressing Forward

Galatians 6:9 (KJV)

"And let us not be weary in well doing: for in due season we shall reap, if we faint not." #1 Don't Get Tired of Honoring God

Honoring God through your actions, service, and obedience can sometimes feel challenging, especially when results aren't immediate. But every effort to live for Him matters. Whether you're loving others, serving in ministry, or standing firm in faith, God sees it all. Don't let fatigue or discouragement keep you from doing what pleases Him. Your persistence honors Him and strengthens your walk with Him.

#2 Honoring God Ushers in Your Season

Every season of sowing leads to a season of reaping. When you honor God consistently, you're planting seeds that will bring a harvest in His perfect timing. The "due season" is a promise of reward and blessing. Trust that your faithfulness is preparing the way for God to move in your life in ways beyond what you can imagine.

#3 Fainting Forfeits Your Season

The temptation to give up often comes right before the breakthrough. Fainting—losing heart or quitting—can cost you the reward God has prepared for you. Stay the course, even when it's hard. Lean on God for strength when you feel weak, and remember that He will carry you through to your harvest if you remain steadfast.

Prayer

Lord, thank You for reminding me that my efforts to
honor You are not in vain. Help me to stay faithful and
not grow weary, trusting in Your perfect timing.
Strengthen me when I feel like giving up, and remind me
of the harvest You have promised. In Jesus' name, Amen.

Reflection Question

What steps can you take today to stay faithful in honoring
God, even when it feels difficult?

Action Question:

How can I serve God today?

_____

_____

_____

_____

Good morning Holy Spirit, will you speak to me today.

Devotional: Marks of the Believer

Galatians 5:13 (KJV)

"For, brethren, ye have been called unto liberty; only use not liberty for an occasion to the flesh, but by love serve one another."

#1 We Walk in Liberty

As believers, we are called to freedom—freedom from sin, guilt, and the law's bondage. This liberty is a gift purchased by Christ's sacrifice. It's not a license to live recklessly but an opportunity to live righteously. Walking in liberty means living in the grace and power God provides to overcome sin and reflect His character.

#2 But We Walk in Love

True liberty is expressed through love. God calls us to walk in love, not selfishness. The love we receive from Him becomes the love we give to others. Walking in love means putting others' needs above our own, extending grace, forgiveness, and kindness. This love becomes the foundation of our relationships and witness to the world.

#3 Then We Live to Serve

The mark of a believer is a life of service. Christ set the example of humble servanthood, and He calls us to do the same. Serving others is how we demonstrate both our liberty and our love. It's not a burden but a joy, knowing that in serving others, we are serving God.

Prayer

Lord, thank You for calling me to liberty and freedom in Christ. Help me to use this freedom not for myself but to love and serve others. Teach me to walk in Your love daily and to live a life that reflects Your heart. In Jesus' name, Amen.

Reflection Question

How can you use your freedom in Christ today to love and serve someone around you?

Action Question:

How can I serve God today?

_____

_____

_____

_____

Good morning Holy Spirit, will you speak to me today.

Devotional: Everyday Bread

Matthew 6:11 (KJV)

"Give us this day our daily bread."

#1 Bread for Life

God is the source of everything we need to sustain us physically, emotionally, and spiritually. The daily bread we ask for represents His provision for our lives. He knows our needs before we ask, and He faithfully supplies them day by day. Trust Him to provide what you need to thrive, knowing He is the ultimate sustainer.

#2 Bread for Hope

Daily bread is more than just sustenance—it's a reminder of God's faithfulness. Each time we rely on Him, our hope is renewed. God's provision today assures us He'll be there tomorrow. As you trust Him for your daily needs, let it fill you with hope for what's ahead. He is the God who never fails to meet us where we are.

#3 Bread for Strength

Life's challenges require more than physical strength; they require spiritual stamina. The bread God gives nourishes not just the body but the soul, empowering us to face every trial with faith and courage. His daily provision strengthens us to keep going, knowing that His grace is sufficient for every moment.

Prayer

Lord, thank You for providing my daily bread—for life, hope, and strength. Help me to trust You each day for what I need and to find joy in Your constant faithfulness. Nourish my body and soul as I walk with You. In Jesus' name, Amen.

Reflection Question

What area of your life do you need to trust God to provide for today? How will you rely on Him for your daily bread?

Action Question:

How can I serve God today?

_____

_____

_____

_____

Good morning Holy Spirit, will you speak to me today.

Devotional: Contend for the Faith

Jude 1:3 (KJV).

"Beloved, when I gave all diligence to write unto you of the common salvation, it was needful for me to write unto you, and exhort you that ye should earnestly contend for the faith which was once delivered unto the saints."

#1 Pour Your All Into What You Believe

Faith isn't passive; it's active. God calls us to wholeheartedly invest in the faith we've received. Pouring your all into your faith means prioritizing God's Word, pursuing His presence, and living out His truths daily. What you believe should shape every part of your life—your choices, actions, and relationships.

#2 The Enemy Is After What You Believe

The enemy's primary strategy is to attack your faith, sowing doubt, discouragement, and distraction. He knows that if he can weaken your belief, he can hinder your purpose. Stay vigilant, guarding your heart and mind with the truth of God's Word. Recognize his schemes and stand firm in the knowledge that your faith is your greatest weapon.

#3 Be Willing to Go to War for What You Believe

Contending for the faith requires courage and perseverance. It means standing firm against opposition, defending the truth, and fighting the good fight of faith. The faith delivered to the saints is worth protecting and proclaiming. Be ready to go to war spiritually, using prayer, the Word, and God's power to remain steadfast in your belief.

Prayer

Lord, thank You for the gift of faith. Help me to pour my all into what I believe, to guard my heart from the enemy's attacks, and to stand firm in the truth. Give me courage to contend for the faith, knowing it is worth the fight. Strengthen me to live boldly for You. In Jesus' name, Amen.

Write two things that stand out from today's scripture?

Reflection Question

How can you actively defend and deepen your faith today in the face of life's challenges?

Action Question:

How can I serve God today?

_____

_____

_____

_____

Good morning Holy Spirit, will you speak to me today.

Devotional: Living in God's Overload

Ephesians 3:20 (KJV)

"Now unto him that is able to do exceeding abundantly above all that we ask or think, according to the power that worketh in us."

#1 God Wants to Overload Your Life

God's desire is to bless you beyond your imagination. He isn't limited by your expectations or requests. His ability to do "exceeding abundantly" means He wants to pour out His goodness, grace, and favor in overwhelming measure. Open your heart to the abundant overflow He has for you.

#2 God Wants Your Life to Be on Overload for Him

God's blessings are not just for you—they're meant to reflect His glory and love to the world. When your life overflows with His presence, others are drawn to Him. Let your blessings—your joy, peace, and faith—be a testimony of His greatness as you live a life fully dedicated to Him.

#3 Overload in Prayer, Worship, and Word

To experience God's exceeding abundance, immerse yourself in prayer, worship, and His Word. These are the channels through which His power flows into your life. Pray boldly, worship passionately, and dive deeply into Scripture. As you overload your life with these spiritual disciplines, God will exceed every expectation.

Prayer

Lord, thank You for being the God of abundance who desires to exceed my greatest expectations. Help me to open my heart to Your overflow and to live fully for You. Teach me to seek You in prayer, worship, and Your Word so that my life reflects Your glory. In Jesus' name, Amen.

Reflection Question

What steps can you take today to position yourself for God's exceeding abundance in prayer, worship, and His Word?

Action Question:

How can I serve God today?

_____

_____

_____

_____

Good morning Holy Spirit, will you speak to me today.

Devotional: God at Work in You

Philippians 2:13 (KJV)

"For it is God which worketh in you both to will and to do of his good pleasure."

#1 Work with God

God is actively working in you, shaping your desires and actions to align with His purpose. Your role is to partner with Him, surrendering your plans and trusting His guidance. Working with God means being intentional about seeking His will and letting His Spirit lead your life.

#2 He'll Hijack Your Will

When you surrender to God, He transforms your heart and desires. The things you once wanted may fade, replaced by a yearning for His ways. God's "hijacking" of your will is not forceful but loving, redirecting you toward the abundant life He has planned. Trust Him to work through your weaknesses and align your will with His.

#3 He'll Assure His Purpose and Pleasure in Your Life

God's work in you guarantees that His purpose will prevail. As you yield to Him, He enables you to live a life that pleases Him and fulfills His plans. His pleasure becomes your greatest joy, and His purpose unfolds beautifully in your obedience. Rest in the assurance that He is faithful to complete His work in you.

Prayer

Lord, thank You for working in me to shape my will and actions for Your glory. Help me to partner with You, surrendering my desires to Your purpose. Redirect my heart and assure Your pleasure in every area of my life. In Jesus' name, Amen.

Reflection Question

How can you intentionally partner with God today to align your will with His purpose?

Action Question:

How can I serve God today?

_____

_____

_____

_____

Good morning Holy Spirit, will you speak to me today.

Devotional: Fighting the Good Fight

1 Timothy 6:12 (KJV)

"Fight the good fight of faith, lay hold on eternal life, whereunto thou art also called, and hast professed a good profession before many witnesses."

#1 Fight with Purpose

Every fight of faith has a purpose—eternal life. The struggles you face as a believer are not random; they are opportunities to strengthen your faith and glorify God. Keep your focus on the ultimate goal: living a life that honors Christ and securing the eternal prize He promises. Purpose gives your fight meaning and direction.

#2 Make It a Faith Fight

Not every battle is worth fighting, but the fight of faith always is. Choose to fight with the tools God provides—His Word, prayer, and trust in His promises. Let your faith be your weapon against fear, doubt, and the enemy's schemes. When faith leads the fight, victory is assured.

#3 Every Faith Fight Is a Good Fight

The fight of faith is never in vain. It's a good fight because it draws you closer to God, builds your character, and secures eternal rewards. Though the fight may feel difficult at times, the outcome is worth every struggle. Trust that God is with you in the battle, and He will see you through to victory.

Prayer

Lord, thank You for calling me to fight the good fight of faith. Help me to fight with purpose, to use faith as my weapon, and to trust that every faith fight is for my good. Strengthen me in the battles I face and remind me of the eternal victory You have promised. In Jesus' name, Amen.

Reflection Question

What battle of faith are you facing today, and how can you fight it with purpose and trust in God?

Action Question:

How can I serve God today?

_____

_____

_____

_____

Good morning Holy Spirit, will you speak to me today.

Devotional: Don't Get Weary

Galatians 6:9 (KJV)

"And let us not be weary in well doing: for in due season we shall reap, if we faint not." #1 Put Aside the Notion to Get Weary

Weariness is a natural response to challenges, but God calls us to rise above it. Remember, you're not walking in your strength alone—God is sustaining you. Put aside the temptation to grow tired by refocusing on His promises and the purpose behind your efforts.

#2 You Are Doing Well

Sometimes we need the reminder that what we're doing matters. Your faithfulness, kindness, and obedience are noticed by God. Even when it feels like no one sees, He sees. Stay encouraged—you are doing well in your pursuit of good.

#3 Weariness Will Lead to Quitting

If unchecked, weariness can cause you to abandon the very work God has called you to do. Don't let the weight of the wait or the struggle cause you to faint. Lean into God's strength, knowing that quitting is not an option when the reward is eternal.

#4 You're Not Waiting on a Blessing but a Season

God's timing is perfect. The blessings He has for you aren't random—they're tied to your due season. Trust that He is preparing everything for its appointed time.

While you wait, keep sowing, keep believing, and keep doing well. Your season is coming.

Prayer

Lord, thank You for the promise of reaping in due season. Help me to put aside weariness and to trust in Your perfect timing. Strengthen me to continue doing well and to wait patiently for the harvest You have prepared. In Jesus' name, Amen.

Reflection Question

How can you stay encouraged and focused while waiting for your due season?

Action Question:

How can I serve God today?

_____

_____

_____

_____

Good morning Holy Spirit, will you speak to me today.

Devotional: Pressing Forward

Philippians 3:13 (KJV)

"Brethren, I count not myself to have apprehended: but this one thing I do, forgetting those things which are behind, and reaching forth unto those things which are before." #1 Know Where You Are

Recognizing where you are in your spiritual journey is key to growth. Paul humbly admitted he hadn't "apprehended" or fully arrived, and neither have we. This acknowledgment isn't defeat—it's an invitation to keep pursuing God's purpose. Stay humble and teachable as you journey forward.

#2 Don't Dwell on the Past

The past, whether filled with victories or failures, can hold you back if you dwell on it. God calls us to release what's behind and focus on what lies ahead. Let go of regrets, disappointments, and even past successes that might hinder your progress. Fix your eyes on the future God has for you.

#3 Put Effort Into What Really Matters

Paul's focus was clear: he put all his energy into reaching for the things of God. Prioritize your time and effort on what has eternal value—knowing God more, living in His purpose, and loving others. The race of faith requires focus, determination, and a forward-thinking mindset.

Prayer

Lord, thank You for the call to keep pressing forward.
Help me to let go of the past and to focus my energy on
what truly matters. Guide me as I pursue Your purpose
for my life, and give me the strength to keep reaching for
what's ahead. In Jesus' name, Amen.

Reflection Question

What is one thing from your past that you need to release
in order to move forward in faith?

Action Question:

How can I serve God today?

_____

_____

_____

_____

Good morning Holy Spirit, will you speak to me today.

Devotional: It Pays to Keep Going

1 Corinthians 15:58 (KJV)

"Therefore, my beloved brethren, be ye steadfast, unmoveable, always abounding in the work of the Lord, forasmuch as ye know that your labour is not in vain in the Lord." #1 Don't Be Moved by the Circumstances

Life often throws obstacles and uncertainties in our path, but as believers, we are called to remain steadfast. Circumstances may change, but God's faithfulness doesn't. Anchor yourself in His promises and stand firm, knowing He is your steady foundation.

#2 Be Persistent in God

God values persistence. Abounding in His work means continuing even when results aren't immediate or visible. Trust that your prayers, service, and obedience are making an eternal impact. When you persevere in God's work, He strengthens and equips you to keep going.

#3 It Pays to Keep Going

The reward for steadfastness and persistence is immeasurable. Your labor is not in vain because God sees and honors your faithfulness. Keep going, knowing that your efforts will yield a harvest in His perfect time. It always pays to remain faithful in the work of the Lord.

Prayer

Lord, thank You for the assurance that my work for You is not in vain. Help me to stand firm when challenges arise and to persist in serving You with joy and commitment. Strengthen my faith and remind me daily that it always pays to keep going. In Jesus' name, Amen.

Reflection Question

What specific areas of your life can you commit to being steadfast and persistent in today?

Action Question:

How can I serve God today?

Good morning Holy Spirit, will you speak to me today.

Devotional: Strength for Every Season

Philippians 4:13 (KJV)

"I can do all things through Christ which strengtheneth me."

#1 Never Underestimate You

Through Christ, you are capable of more than you realize. God has equipped you with talents, resilience, and purpose. Don't downplay your ability to rise above challenges or accomplish great things—because with Christ, your potential knows no bounds.

#2 Never Distrust the God in You

The same power that raised Christ from the dead lives in you. Trust in God's presence and power within you to guide, strengthen, and equip you for every challenge. Lean into His promises, and watch how He works through you in extraordinary ways.

#3 His Strength Is Unending

God's strength has no limits, and He generously pours it out to those who rely on Him. Whether you're feeling weak, overwhelmed, or unqualified, remember that His power is perfected in your weakness. Through Him, you have unending strength for whatever lies ahead.

Prayer

Lord, thank You for the strength You provide through Christ. Help me to never underestimate what You can do in me, to always trust in Your power, and to rely on Your unending strength in every situation. In Jesus' name, Amen.

Reflection Question

How can you lean into God's strength today to accomplish something you feel unprepared for?

Action Question:

How can I serve God today?

_____

_____

_____

_____

Good morning Holy Spirit, will you speak to me today.

Devotional: Personal Praise

Psalm 8:2 (KJV)

"Out of the mouth of babes and sucklings hast thou ordained strength because of thine enemies, that thou mightest still the enemy and the avenger."

#1 Personal Praise Is the Result of Dependence on God

True praise flows from a heart that relies on God completely. Like a child depending on their parent, our acknowledgment of God's sovereignty and provision leads to a personal and authentic expression of gratitude and worship. When you depend on Him, your praise becomes a natural response.

#2 Personal Praise Results in Strength

God ordains strength through our praise. When we exalt Him, we exchange our weakness for His power. Praise builds spiritual resilience, renewing your spirit and preparing you to face whatever challenges come your way.

#3 Personal Praise Renders Your Enemy Powerless

Your praise is a weapon that silences the enemy. When you lift your voice in worship, it confuses and dismantles the plans of the adversary. Your personal praise reminds the enemy that God is in control and that victory is already yours through Christ.

Prayer

Lord, I depend on You for everything, and I offer You my personal praise. Strengthen me through worship, and let my praise silence every attack of the enemy. May my heart always reflect my trust in You. In Jesus' name, Amen.

Reflection Question

How can you make personal praise a daily practice to strengthen your walk with God and overcome challenges?

Action Question:

How can I serve God today?

_____

_____

_____

_____

Good morning Holy Spirit, will you speak to me today.

Devotional: Knowing God, Knowing Victory

2 Corinthians 2:14 (KJV)

"Now thanks be unto God, which always causeth us to triumph in Christ, and maketh manifest the savour of his knowledge by us in every place."

#1 Know God, Know Victory

Victory begins with knowing God. When you cultivate a deep relationship with Him, you step into the triumph that comes through Christ. No matter the challenges, you can trust that God's plan is to lead you into victory every time. Knowing Him is knowing that defeat is not your portion.

#2 Know God, Show Victory

Your life is a reflection of God's triumph. As you walk in His victory, His presence in you becomes evident to others. You carry the fragrance of His knowledge wherever you go, demonstrating the power and goodness of God to a watching world. Victory is not just for you—it's a testimony to those around you.

Prayer

Lord, thank You for always causing me to triumph in Christ. Help me to know You more deeply so I can walk confidently in the victory You provide. Let my life be a reflection of Your power and grace, pointing others to You. In Jesus' name, Amen.

Reflection Question

How can you deepen your relationship with God to experience and share His victory in every area of your life?

Action Question:

How can I serve God today?

_____

_____

_____

_____

Good morning Holy Spirit, will you speak to me today.

Devotional: Choosing Christ in Every Moment

John 16:33 (KJV)

"These things I have spoken unto you, that in me ye might have peace. In the world ye shall have tribulation: but be of good cheer; I have overcome the world."

#1 In Peace, Choose Christ

Peace begins with choosing Christ. In every situation, good or bad, He is the constant source of calm and assurance. By prioritizing His presence and guidance, you find a peace that the world cannot give. Choose Christ daily, and experience His steady hand in all things.

#2 In Tribulation, Still Choose Christ

Life's tribulations are inevitable, but they don't have to rob you of your joy or faith. Even in the toughest seasons, choose Christ. He is your refuge, your strength, and your peace. Lean on Him, trusting that He is bigger than any challenge you face.

#3 Christ Has Already Chosen You

Your choice to follow Christ is only possible because He first chose you. He overcame the world, securing victory for you. His love and sacrifice prove that He is fully committed to you. Knowing this, you can confidently walk in His peace and victory.

Prayer

Lord, thank You for being my peace in every circumstance. Help me to choose You in every moment, especially in times of tribulation. Thank You for overcoming the world and for choosing me to walk in Your love and victory. In Jesus' name, Amen.

Reflection Question

How can you choose Christ today in both the small and challenging moments of your life?

Action Question:

How can I serve God today?

_____

_____

_____

_____

Good morning Holy Spirit, will you speak to me today.

Devotional: Stay in the Flow of Prayer

Colossians 4:2 (KJV)

"Continue in prayer, and watch in the same with thanksgiving."

#1 Pray While You Move

Prayer isn't confined to a specific place or moment—it's a lifestyle. As you go about your day, keep the lines of communication open with God. Whether you're walking, working, or waiting, take everything to Him in prayer, knowing He's always listening.

#2 Watch While You Pray

Prayer and awareness go hand in hand. Be spiritually alert, looking for how God is moving and working in your life and the lives of others. Stay sensitive to His guidance and protection, knowing He answers in His perfect timing.

#3 Stay grateful

Thanksgiving should always accompany your prayers. Gratitude shifts your perspective, reminding you of God's faithfulness and provision. No matter the situation, there's always a reason to give thanks—because God is good and His love endures forever.

Prayer

Lord, teach me to pray without ceasing and to remain watchful for Your hand in every situation. Fill my heart with gratitude so that my prayers are always surrounded by thanksgiving. Thank You for hearing and answering me. In Jesus' name, Amen.

Reflection Question

How can you incorporate prayer, vigilance, and thanksgiving into your daily routine today?

Action Question:

How can I serve God today?

_____

_____

_____

_____

Good morning Holy Spirit, will you speak to me today.

Devotional: The Gifts of God's Presence

Psalm 16:11 (KJV)

"Thou wilt shew me the path of life: in thy presence is fullness of joy; at thy right hand there are pleasures for evermore."

#1 God Will Give You Clarity

Life's path can be unclear, but God promises to guide you. In His presence, He reveals the way you should go, providing wisdom and direction for every decision. Trust Him to illuminate your steps and lead you on the path of life.

#2 God Will Give You Joy

True, lasting joy is found in the presence of the Lord. It's not tied to circumstances but flows from His unchanging goodness and love. When you dwell with Him, you experience a joy that fills every corner of your soul.

#3 God Will Give You a Good Life

At God's right hand are eternal pleasures—blessings that satisfy both now and forever. Walking with Him leads to a life rich in peace, purpose, and fulfillment. He desires to give you more than just existence—He offers an abundant and good life.

Prayer

Lord, thank You for being the source of my clarity, joy, and good life. Help me to stay close to Your presence and trust Your guidance. Fill me with joy that sustains and blesses me with the abundant life You've promised. In Jesus' name, Amen.

Reflection Question

How can you seek God's presence today for clarity, joy, and a more fulfilling life?

Action Question:

How can I serve God today?

_____

_____

_____

_____

Good morning Holy Spirit, will you speak to me today.

Devotional: Living with Hope and Prayer

Romans 12:12 (KJV)

"Rejoicing in hope; patient in tribulation; continuing instant in prayer."

#1 Spirit of Expectation

Hope fuels your joy. As believers, we live with the confident expectation that God will fulfill His promises. Rejoice in the hope that God is working everything together for your good, and let that hope ignite your faith and brighten your outlook.

#2 Heart of Endurance

Tribulation is inevitable, but patience in hard times shows your trust in God's timing. Endurance is cultivated when you anchor yourself in His Word and trust His plan. Stay steadfast, knowing the trials are temporary, but God's promises are eternal.

#3 Mind to Engage God

Prayer is your lifeline to God. A mind constantly engaging with Him invites peace, guidance, and strength. Make prayer your first response, not your last resort. Stay connected to God through continual conversation, and watch Him move in every area of your life.

Prayer

Lord, I rejoice in the hope You've given me, and I trust You through every trial. Help me to endure with patience and to always seek You in prayer. May my life reflect a heart of expectation, perseverance, and dependence on You. In Jesus' name, Amen.

Reflection Question

How can you incorporate hope, patience, and consistent prayer into your daily walk with God today?

Action Question:

How can I serve God today?

_____

_____

_____

_____

Good morning Holy Spirit, will you speak to me today.

Devotional: Run to Win

1 Corinthians 9:24 (KJV)

"Know ye not that they which run in a race run all, but one receiveth the prize? So run, that ye may obtain."

#1 Determine You Are the Winner

Winning starts with the right mindset. In Christ, you are already victorious. When you step into the race of life, declare that you are running with purpose and determination. Believe that God has equipped you to win.

#2 Prepare to Win

Winners prepare. Just as athletes train and discipline themselves, you must prepare spiritually. Stay grounded in prayer, study the Word, and live a life of faith and obedience. Your preparation is key to finishing strong.

#3 Go Win

Winning requires action. Run your race with all your strength, knowing the prize is eternal. Keep your eyes on the goal, and don't let distractions or setbacks deter you. In Christ, you have everything you need to cross the finish line victoriously.

Prayer

Lord, thank You for calling me to run this race with purpose. Help me to believe in the victory You've promised, prepare with diligence, and run with endurance. Strengthen me to finish well and obtain the prize You've set before me. In Jesus' name, Amen.

Reflection Question

What steps can you take today to prepare for and run the
race God has set before you?

Action Question:

How can I serve God today?

Good morning Holy Spirit, will you speak to me today.

Devotional: Faith Beyond Sight

John 20:29 (KJV)

"Jesus saith unto him, Thomas, because thou hast seen me, thou hast believed: blessed are they that have not seen, and yet have believed." #1 Seeing Is Not Always Believing

Faith doesn't rely on physical proof. While Thomas believed after seeing, Jesus calls us to a deeper trust—a faith that believes even when we don't see. True faith rests not in sight but in the assurance of God's promises.

#2 Learn to Believe for What You Don't See

Faith challenges us to trust in what hasn't yet materialized. Whether it's a promise, a breakthrough, or God's plan for your life, believing without seeing strengthens your spiritual walk and aligns you with God's greater purpose.

#3 Your Future Is in What You Believe

What you believe shapes your future. When you place your faith in God, you step into His plans and promises. Your destiny isn't defined by what you see now but by the unseen realities of His Word and His will for your life.

Prayer

Lord, help me to believe even when I don't see. Strengthen my faith to trust Your Word and Your promises. Let my confidence in You shape my future and bring glory to Your name. In Jesus' name, Amen.

Reflection Question

What is one area in your life where God is calling you to trust Him without seeing?

Action Question:

How can I serve God today?

_____

_____

_____

_____

Good morning Holy Spirit, will you speak to me today.

Devotional: Joy in the Trial

James 1:2-3 (KJV)

"My brethren, count it all joy when ye fall into divers temptations; Knowing this, that the trying of your faith worketh patience." #1 Your Trial Won't Take You Out

Trials may feel overwhelming, but they are not designed to destroy you. God uses every challenge to strengthen your faith and deepen your reliance on Him. Trust that He's with you and that this trial will not be the end of your story.

#2 Your Patience Gets a Workout

Every trial is an opportunity for growth. As your faith is tested, your patience is being refined and stretched. This process builds endurance, equipping you to handle greater challenges and responsibilities in God's plan for your life.

#3 Declare Your Joy

Joy is a choice, even in the midst of trials. When you count it all joy, you're declaring that God is in control and that He will bring you through stronger. Let joy be your declaration of faith, knowing that the outcome is in His hands.

Prayer

Lord, thank You for being with me through every trial. Help me to see challenges as opportunities to grow and trust You more. Give me the strength to choose joy, knowing that You are working all things for my good. In Jesus' name, Amen.

Reflection Question

How can you declare joy in your current challenges, trusting God's purpose in your trials?

Action Question:

How can I serve God today?

Good morning Holy Spirit, will you speak to me today.

Devotional: Guard Your Heart

Proverbs 4:23 (KJV)

"Keep thy heart with all diligence; for out of it are the issues of life."

#1 Your Heart Must Be Protected

Your heart is the core of who you are. It influences your thoughts, emotions, and decisions. Protect it from negativity, sin, and anything that seeks to pull you away from God's purpose. A guarded heart remains aligned with God's will.

#2 Protect It at All Cost

Guarding your heart requires intentionality. Be mindful of what you allow into your life through relationships, media, and conversations. Set boundaries that prioritize your spiritual well-being. Your heart is too valuable to leave unguarded.

#3 It's the Source of Life

Everything flows from your heart—your dreams, faith, and purpose. When your heart is rooted in God, your life reflects His love and truth. Keep your heart connected to Him, and you will live out the abundant life He has promised.

Prayer

Lord, help me to guard my heart with diligence. Protect it from anything that does not honor You and fill it with Your love, wisdom, and peace. Let my life reflect the purity of a heart that belongs to You. In Jesus' name, Amen.

Reflection Question

What steps can you take today to better guard your heart and keep it aligned with God's will?

Action Question:

How can I serve God today?

_____

_____

_____

_____

Good morning Holy Spirit, will you speak to me today.

Devotional: Living the Best Life

Romans 12:12 (KJV)

"Rejoicing in hope; patient in tribulation; continuing instant in prayer."

#1 Live in Confidence

Hope is the foundation of your joy. When you place your confidence in God's promises, you can rejoice no matter the circumstances. Living the best life begins with trusting that God has a plan and that His plan is always good.

#2 Live in Steadfast Faith

Tribulation is a part of life, but patience in trials reflects your steadfast faith. By holding on to God's Word and remaining faithful, you'll grow stronger and more resilient. Your endurance will produce a deeper trust in Him.

#3 Live Devoted to Prayer

A life devoted to prayer is a life connected to God. Continual prayer keeps your heart aligned with His will and invites His presence into every area of your life. When you make prayer a priority, you'll experience peace, guidance, and strength.

Prayer

Lord, help me to live my best life by rejoicing in Your hope, trusting You in trials, and staying connected to You through prayer. Let my confidence, faith, and devotion glorify You in all that I do. In Jesus' name, Amen.

Reflection Question

What steps can you take today to live a life of confidence, faith, and prayer?

Action Question:

How can I serve God today?

_____

_____

_____

_____

Good morning Holy Spirit, will you speak to me today.

Devotional: Hold What You Got

Hebrews 10:23 (KJV)

"Let us hold fast the profession of our faith without wavering; (for he is faithful that promised.)"

#1 Don't Let Impatience Make You Move

Waiting can be difficult, but God's timing is perfect. Trust Him even when the answer or breakthrough seems delayed. Impatience can cause you to step outside of His will, but holding fast keeps you aligned with His promises.

#2 Don't Let People Make You Move

Voices around you might challenge your faith or try to influence your decisions. Stay anchored in God's truth. Remember, your faith is in Him, not in the opinions or actions of others.

#3 Don't Let Pressure Make You Move

Trials and challenges can press hard on your faith, but don't let them shake you. Pressure is temporary, but God's promises are eternal. Stand firm, knowing He is working on your behalf.

#4 Hold Fast in the Promise

God's faithfulness is the foundation of your hope. Cling tightly to His promises, knowing that He never fails. His Word assures you that what He has spoken will come to pass.

Prayer

Lord, give me the strength to hold fast to my faith no matter what comes my way. Help me to resist impatience, distractions, and pressure, trusting fully in Your faithfulness. I stand on Your promises, knowing that You will bring them to fulfillment. In Jesus' name, Amen.

Reflection Question

What steps can you take today to hold fast to your faith despite challenges or delays?

Action Question:

How can I serve God today?

Good morning Holy Spirit, will you speak to me today.

Devotional: Keep HIM Close

Psalm 22:3 (KJV)

"But thou art holy, O thou that inhabitest the praises of Israel."

#1 Worry Is Not the Answer

Worry creates distance between you and God by focusing on fear rather than faith. Instead of dwelling on what could go wrong, redirect your thoughts toward His promises. Trust that God is already working on your behalf.

#2 Words (Complaining) Are Not the Answer

Complaining shifts your focus to the problem, not the Provider. Negative words can disrupt your spirit and hinder your faith. Instead, choose to speak life and declare God's goodness, even in difficult situations.

#3 Worship Keeps HIM Close

God inhabits the praises of His people. When you worship, you invite His presence into your life. Worship shifts your focus from the challenge to the One who holds the solution. Stay close to Him by lifting up your voice in praise.

Prayer

Lord, help me to replace worry with worship and complaints with praise. I draw near to You, knowing that Your presence brings peace, guidance, and strength. Let

my life be a reflection of faith and gratitude. In Jesus'
name, Amen.

Reflection Question

How can you replace worry and complaining with
worship today?

Action Question:

How can I serve God today?

_____

_____

_____

_____

Good morning Holy Spirit, will you speak to me today.

Devotional: Be the Blessing

Ephesians 2:10 (KJV)

"For we are his workmanship, created in Christ Jesus unto good works, which God hath before ordained that we should walk in them."

#1 You Were Created to Be a Blessing

God made you uniquely and intentionally for a purpose. You are His masterpiece, designed to reflect His goodness and love. Being a blessing is not just something you do; it's who you are in Christ.

#2 You Have the Ability to Be a Blessing

God has equipped you with gifts, talents, and opportunities to bless others. Whether through kind words, acts of service, or simply showing love, you have everything you need to make a difference in someone's life.

#3 Be a Blessing No Matter What

Life's challenges can make it hard to focus on helping others, but don't let circumstances stop you. When you bless others, you reflect God's love and open the door for His blessings to flow through you and to you.

Prayer

Lord, thank You for creating me with a purpose to do good works. Help me to see every opportunity to be a blessing and give me the strength to serve others regardless of my circumstances. Let my life glorify You. In Jesus' name, Amen.

Reflection Question

How can you intentionally be a blessing to someone today?

Action Question:

How can I serve God today?

_____

_____

_____

_____

Good morning Holy Spirit, will you speak to me today.

Devotional: Fearless and Strong

Deuteronomy 31:6 (KJV)

"Be strong and of a good courage, fear not, nor be afraid of them: for the LORD thy God, he it is that doth go with thee; he will not fail thee, nor forsake thee."

#1 Your Strength Is in Your God

True strength doesn't come from your abilities but from the One who goes with you. God's power is unlimited, and His presence ensures you have all you need to face every challenge. Lean on Him, and His strength will sustain you.

#2 Your Courage Cancels Your Fear

Courage is not the absence of fear but the choice to trust God in the face of it. When you step out in faith, fear loses its grip. Boldly confront every obstacle, knowing that God is greater than any challenge you face.

#3 Your God Is Always There

God's promise to never fail or forsake you is unchanging. No matter what you're going through, He is with you, guiding and protecting you. His presence is your constant source of peace and assurance.

Prayer

Lord, thank You for being my strength and courage. Help me to trust in Your presence and promises, knowing that You will never leave me. With You, I can face anything without fear. In Jesus' name, Amen.

Reflection Question

How can you rely on God's strength and courage to overcome a current fear or challenge?

Action Question:

How can I serve God today?

_____

_____

_____

_____

Good morning Holy Spirit, will you speak to me today.

Devotional: Wait on the Lord

Psalm 40:1-2 (KJV)

"I waited patiently for the LORD; and he inclined unto me, and heard my cry. He brought me up also out of a horrible pit, out of the miry clay, and set my feet upon a rock, and established my goings."

#1 Wait: Relationship Is Taking Place (He Inclines His Ear)

In the waiting, God draws near to you. His ear is attentive to your prayers, and His presence surrounds you. Waiting isn't passive; it's a moment to deepen your relationship with Him, knowing He is listening with love.

#2 Wait: Intimacy Is Taking Place (He Heard My Cry)

God doesn't just hear your words—He hears your heart. In the quiet moments of waiting, He connects with your deepest needs, offering comfort and assurance. Trust that your cries have reached the One who cares most.

#3 Wait: He's Changing My Situation (Brought Me Out)

God works in His perfect timing to lift you out of difficulties. The waiting season may feel long, but it's where He prepares the breakthrough. He's not just moving on your behalf—He's bringing transformation to your situation.

#4 Wait: He's Creating Me a Future (Establish My Goings)

God's plans for you are secure. As you wait, He's setting your path and establishing your steps. The future He's shaping is one of purpose, stability, and hope. Trust Him to guide you into what's next.

Prayer

Lord, help me to wait on You with patience and faith. Thank You for drawing near to me, hearing my prayers, and working in my life. I trust that in Your timing, You will bring me out and establish my steps. In Jesus' name, Amen.

Reflection Question

How can you trust God more during your waiting season, knowing He's working for your good?

Action Question:

How can I serve God today?

_____

_____

_____

_____

Good morning Holy Spirit, will you speak to me today.

Devotional: Look Up

Psalm 121:1-2 (KJV)

"I will lift up mine eyes unto the hills, from whence cometh my help. My help cometh from the LORD, which made heaven and earth." #1 He'll Heal You

Looking up to God means acknowledging Him as your healer. He is ready to restore your heart, mind, and body. No matter the pain or struggle, His power is greater than any wound you carry. Trust Him for complete healing.

#2 He'll Hold You

God is your constant support. When life feels overwhelming, His presence will sustain you. As you lift your eyes, remember that His arms are strong enough to carry you through any storm. You are never alone.

#3 He'll Help You

Your help comes from the Creator of heaven and earth. He knows exactly what you need and when you need it. Look up with confidence, knowing that He is your source of strength, wisdom, and provision.

Prayer

Lord, I lift my eyes to You, knowing that my help comes from You alone. Thank You for healing me, holding me, and helping me through every situation. Teach me to rely on You more each day. In Jesus' name, Amen.

Reflection Question

What situation do you need to lift to God today and trust Him to heal, hold, or help you?

Action Question:

How can I serve God today?

_____

_____

_____

_____

Good morning Holy Spirit, will you speak to me today.

Devotional: It's Not Too Hard

Jeremiah 32:17 (KJV)

"Ah Lord GOD! behold, thou hast made the heaven and the earth by thy great power and stretched out arm, and there is nothing too hard for thee."

#1 God Does Not Struggle to Keep His Promises

The Creator of heaven and earth does not wrestle with fulfilling His word. His great power ensures that every promise He has made is certain to come to pass. Trust that He is faithful and capable of doing exactly what He said.

#2 Answering Prayer Is What He Does

God specializes in hearing and responding to the cries of His people. No prayer is too big, and no detail is too small. Lay your requests before Him, knowing that answering your needs is part of His loving nature.

#3 There's No Problem Too Tough for Him

Whether the mountain seems immovable or the valley too deep, God's power surpasses every obstacle. He is the God of the impossible. Trust Him with every challenge, knowing nothing is too hard for Him.

Prayer

Lord, thank You for being the God of the impossible. I trust You to fulfill Your promises, answer my prayers, and handle every challenge I face. Help me to rest in Your great power and faithfulness. In Jesus' name, Amen.

Reflection Question

What tough situation can you surrender to God today,
trusting that it is not too hard for Him?

Action Question:

How can I serve God today?

_____

_____

_____

_____

Good morning Holy Spirit, will you speak to me today.

Devotional: Press

Philippians 3:14 (KJV)

"I press toward the mark for the prize of the high calling of God in Christ Jesus."

#1 Pressing Suggests Resistance

The journey toward God's calling is not without challenges. Resistance often comes in the form of obstacles, setbacks, and distractions. Pressing forward means you're willing to push past those difficulties, trusting God to help you overcome.

#2 Pressing Produces Strength

Each step forward, no matter how hard, builds spiritual endurance. The more you press, the stronger you become in faith, character, and determination. God uses the process to shape and prepare you for the prize.

#3 Pressing Gets You to Your Destination

The prize of God's high calling is worth the effort. Pressing keeps your focus on Him and ensures you don't stop short of His purpose for your life. Keep your eyes on the goal and trust Him to guide you to victory.

Prayer

Lord, help me to press forward, even when I face resistance. Strengthen me for the journey and keep my focus on Your high calling. I trust that the prize You have for me is worth the press. In Jesus' name, Amen.

Reflection Question

What resistance are you facing today, and how can you
press through it with God's help?

Action Question:

How can I serve God today?

_____

_____

_____

_____

Good morning Holy Spirit, will you speak to me today.

Devotional: You're on God's Mind

Jeremiah 29:11 (KJV)

"For I know the thoughts that I think toward you, saith the LORD, thoughts of peace, and not of evil, to give you an expected end."

#1 You Are on God's Mind

It's humbling to realize that the Almighty God actively thinks about you. He's aware of your circumstances, dreams, and struggles. You are not forgotten or overlooked. Let this truth fill you with hope and confidence: the Creator of the universe is mindful of you personally.

#2 God's Thoughts Are What Matter

Opinions, doubts, and criticism may swirl around you, but God's perspective is the one that truly counts. His thoughts are rooted in truth and love. Seek to align your heart and mind with His Word and His promises. When you do, you'll find clarity and purpose.

#3 His Thoughts Will Result in Peace

God's plans for you are anchored in peace, not chaos. Even when life feels uncertain, you can trust that He is working behind the scenes to bring about good. Rest in the assurance that He offers peace that surpasses all understanding—peace the world cannot provide.

#4 The End Will Be in Your Favor

God promises an expected end—a future and a hope. This doesn't mean life will be free of challenges, but it does mean victory is certain. As you trust His plans and follow His leading, He will guide you into a destiny marked by His goodness and blessing.

Prayer

Lord, thank You for thinking of me and having plans of peace for my life. Help me to focus on Your thoughts rather than the world's opinions. Lead me into the future You have prepared, and fill me with the peace that comes from trusting in You. In Jesus' name, Amen.

Reflection Question

How can you remind yourself today that God's thoughts toward you are good and that your future is secure in His hands?

Action Question:

How can I serve God today?

_____

_____

_____

_____

Good morning Holy Spirit, will you speak to me today.

Devotional: Not Today

1 Corinthians 10:13 (KJV)

"There hath no temptation taken you but such as is common to man: but God is faithful, who will not suffer you to be tempted above that ye are able; but will with the temptation also make a way to escape, that ye may be able to bear it."

#1 Temptations Are Common

Every believer faces temptations—it's a universal human experience. You're not alone in the struggle. Recognizing that temptations are common can free you from shame and remind you that with God's help, you can overcome.

#2 God's Faithfulness Is Constant

In the midst of temptation, God remains unwavering in His faithfulness. He knows your limits and will not allow you to be tested beyond what you can handle. Trust His character; He is your constant source of strength and guidance.

#3 Your Winning Is Consistent

God always provides a way of escape. You're not doomed to fail; victory is within reach when you lean on Him. Keep your eyes on His faithfulness, and each time temptation arises, declare: "Not today!"

Prayer

Lord, thank You for Your faithfulness and for providing a way out of every temptation I face. Help me to remember that I'm not alone and that You are my strength. May I walk in victory each day, trusting You to guide me. In Jesus' name, Amen

Reflection Question

What practical steps can you take today to recognize God's way of escape and choose victory over temptation?

Action Question:

How can I serve God today?

_____

_____

_____

_____

Good morning Holy Spirit, will you speak to me today.

Devotional: Presence with Power

Exodus 33:15 (KJV)

"And he said unto him, If thy presence go not with me, carry us not up hence."

#1 Never Underestimate the Power of God's Presence

Moses understood that God's presence was essential—not optional. He refused to move forward without it. God's presence brings guidance, comfort, and power. It changes atmospheres and transforms hearts. Trust that wherever He leads, His power will sustain you.

#2 Always Set Aside Time for His Presence

If you want to experience God's presence, you must prioritize it. Make time in your daily routine—through prayer, worship, and reading His Word—to seek Him intentionally. In those moments, you'll encounter the fullness of His character and receive the strength you need for every challenge.

#3 The View of Life Changes Through His Presence

When you dwell with God, your perspective shifts. Fear is replaced by faith, anxiety by peace, and confusion by clarity. In His presence, you gain the confidence to face life's uncertainties, knowing He is with you and has everything under control.

Prayer

Lord, I never want to take a step without You. Remind me daily to seek Your presence and to trust in Your power.

Change my perspective as I draw near to You, and help me move forward with confidence and faith. In Jesus' name, Amen.

Reflection Question

How can you intentionally make room in your schedule this week to experience more of God's presence and power?

Action Question:

How can I serve God today?

_____

_____

_____

_____

Good morning Holy Spirit, will you speak to me today.

Devotional: Victory

Romans 8:37 (KJV)

"Nay, in all these things we are more than conquerors through him that loved us."

#1 "Nope" – I Object, I'm an Exception

When challenges arise, remind yourself that you are not the world's exception to defeat. Instead, you're God's exception to the rule of failure. Whatever trial comes your way, declare "Nope!" because in Christ, your story doesn't end in defeat but in victory.

#2 "None" of These Things Will Overtake Me

No hardship, fear, or obstacle can overshadow God's power in your life. With Christ, every challenge must bow to His authority. Stand firm, knowing that none of these things can truly conquer you. You are secure in the One who conquered sin and death.

#3 "Now" – Jesus Is on My Side

Victory is not just a future hope; it's a present reality. The risen Savior who loves you is actively working on your behalf. Whatever you're facing now, remember that Jesus stands beside you, fighting for you, and ensuring you are more than a conqueror.

Prayer

Lord, thank You for making me an exception to defeat through Your power. Remind me daily that no trial can overtake me and that You are on my side right now. Help me to live in the reality of Your victory. In Jesus' name, Amen.

Reflection Question

How can you remind yourself today that you are "more than a conqueror" in Christ, no matter the circumstances you face?

Action Question:

How can I serve God today?

_____

_____

_____

_____

Good morning Holy Spirit, will you speak to me today.

Devotional: Seek Him

Psalm 9:10 (KJV)

"And they that know thy name will put their trust in thee: for thou, LORD, hast not forsaken them that seek thee."

#1 We Seek Him Because We Know Him

When you truly know who God is—His character, His love, and His faithfulness—you can't help but seek Him. Understanding His nature draws you into a deeper relationship. The more you know Him, the more you desire His presence.

#2 We Seek Him Because We Trust Him

Trust grows from knowing God's faithfulness. When life is uncertain, remember who He is and what He's done. Your confidence in His promises will propel you to seek Him even more, knowing He has never failed you yet.

#3 We Seek Him Because He Won't Fail

God's record of faithfulness is perfect. He never forsakes those who earnestly seek Him. No matter what storms arise, He remains the unshakable rock. Seek Him with the assurance that He is your refuge and will not let you down.

Prayer

Lord, thank You for being a faithful God who never forsakes those who seek You. Help me to know You more deeply, trust You more fully, and rest in Your unfailing love. Remind me daily that You will never fail me. In Jesus' name, Amen.

Reflection Question

In what ways can you intentionally seek God today, trusting Him to reveal Himself and prove His faithfulness once again?

Action Question:

How can I serve God today?

_____

_____

_____

_____

Good morning Holy Spirit, will you speak to me today.

Devotional: No Fear

Psalm 56:3–4 (KJV)

"What time I am afraid, I will trust in thee. In God I will praise his word, in God I have put my trust; I will not fear what flesh can do unto me."

#1 Life Has a Tendency to Cause Fear

Fear often creeps in through uncertainties and challenges. Whether it's a new situation or an ongoing struggle, life can stir up anxiety in our hearts. Recognize that moments of fear do happen—but they don't have to define you.

#2 God's Word Has a Tendency to Drive Out Fear

When fear arises, God's Word is your refuge. It reminds you of His promises, His power, and His unfailing love. Meditating on Scripture dispels the lies that anxiety tries to plant. As you praise His Word, your heart becomes anchored in truth, and fear loses its grip.

#3 Trust in God Has a Tendency to Make You Bold

Trusting God shifts your focus from the size of your problem to the greatness of your God. As you place your confidence in Him, boldness replaces apprehension. You realize that no matter what comes against you, God's presence and protection are greater.

Prayer

Lord, when fear tries to grip my heart, help me to remember Your Word and trust in You. Let Your truth drive out every worry, and let my faith in You make me bold. Thank You for being my refuge and strength in all circumstances. In Jesus' name, Amen.

Reflection Question

How can you use God's Word today to replace fearful thoughts with bold trust in His promises

Action Question:

How can I serve God today?

_____

_____

_____

_____

Good morning Holy Spirit, will you speak to me today.

Devotional: Your Mouth

Proverbs 18:20 (KJV)

"A man's belly shall be satisfied with the fruit of his mouth; and with the increase of his lips shall he be filled."

#1 What Fills You Won't Always Satisfy You

We often chase things—status, material possessions, fleeting pleasures—to fill a void. However, these external sources rarely bring true satisfaction. What we take in can temporarily fill us, but it doesn't always meet the deeper need of our soul.

#2 What Satisfies You Is the Fruit of Your Mouth

Scripture teaches us that our words carry weight. The way we speak—our attitudes, confessions, and praises—has the power to bring genuine satisfaction. Positive, faith-filled words can nourish our spirit, while negative words leave us empty. Choose your words wisely, for they shape your outlook and your heart.

#3 Let Your Mouth Produce Satisfying Fruit

Decide today to speak life, hope, and faith. Compliment someone, share an encouraging word, or declare God's promises over your situation. When your words align with God's truth, you cultivate a harvest of inner peace and genuine fulfillment.

Prayer

Lord, help me to be mindful of my words, knowing they carry the power to bring satisfaction or emptiness. Teach me to speak life, hope, and truth in every situation. May my mouth produce fruit that honors You and nourishes my soul. In Jesus' name, Amen.

Reflection Question

What words can you speak today that will bring life and genuine satisfaction to yourself and those around you?

Action Question:

How can I serve God today?

_____

_____

_____

_____

Good morning Holy Spirit, will you speak to me today.

Devotional: Take the Name

Exodus 20:7 (KJV)

"Thou shalt not take the name of the LORD thy God in vain; for the LORD will not hold him guiltless that taketh his name in vain." #1 Take the Name (Identity)

Taking the Lord's name isn't just about speaking it; it's about identifying yourself with who He is. When you call yourself a follower of Christ, you attach His reputation to your life. It's a privilege to "take" His name because you are declaring that you belong to Him and that His character marks your own.

#2 Carry the Name (Live It)

Words are empty if not backed by action. Carrying God's name means living in a way that reflects His holiness, love, and truth. It's not about being perfect but about striving to live according to His standards. Let your daily choices show that you carry the Lord's name with honor.

#3 Don't Embarrass the Name

When you bear God's name, you represent Him to the world. Misusing God's name goes beyond language—it's dishonoring who He is through careless or sinful actions. Aim to walk in integrity so that your life never brings reproach to the name you've taken and carry.

Prayer

Lord, thank You for the privilege of bearing Your name.
Help me to live in a way that honors You and reflects
Your holiness. Guide my words, actions, and thoughts so
that I never misuse or dishonor Your name. In Jesus'
name, Amen.

Reflection Question

What steps can you take today to ensure your life reflects
the honor and holiness of the name you carry?

Action Question:

How can I serve God today?

_____

_____

_____

_____

Good morning Holy Spirit, will you speak to me today.

Devotional: Complete in Him

Colossians 2:9–10 (KJV)

"For in him dwelleth all the fulness of the Godhead bodily. And ye are complete in him, which is the head of all principality and power."

#1 He Fills You

In Jesus, all the fullness of God dwells. When you receive Him, you're not inviting just a portion of God into your life—you're inviting the very fullness of His presence and power. His Spirit fills every gap, every broken place, and every longing of your heart. No area of your life remains untouched when the fullness of Christ resides within you.

#2 He Completes You

You are complete in Him. All your searching for purpose and identity finds its answer in Christ. His love and grace bring wholeness in ways that people, achievements, and possessions never can. Stop striving to fill your life with temporary fixes. Instead, rest in the completeness that He offers.

#3 He Qualifies You

As the head of all principality and power, Jesus rules over every authority, seen and unseen. When you are in Christ, He becomes your qualification. You don't need to prove yourself worthy—He has already done that. His victory over every power means you can walk in confidence, knowing He has made you worthy to stand before God.

Prayer

Lord, thank You for filling my life with Your presence, completing every part of me, and qualifying me through Your finished work. Help me to rest in the fullness of who You are and trust that in You, I have all I need. In Jesus' name, Amen.

Reflection Question

Where in your life do you need to remember and rely on the truth that you are already complete in Christ?

Action Question:

How can I serve God today?

_____

_____

_____

_____

Good morning Holy Spirit, will you speak to me today.

Devotional: It's Still Working

Romans 8:28 (KJV)

"And we know that all things work together for good to them that love God, to them who are called according to his purpose." #1 It's Working in You

Life's challenges and triumphs are tools God uses to shape and refine your character. Even the parts of your story that seem painful or confusing can serve a divine purpose in molding you into the image of Christ. Trust that He's using every circumstance to work in your heart and transform you from the inside out.

#2 It's Working for You

God is not only at work within you, but He's also aligning circumstances for your good. The situations that look like setbacks today can become the very setup for blessings tomorrow. Because you love God and are called according to His purpose, He orchestrates every detail for your ultimate benefit, even when you can't see it yet.

#3 It's Working for His Purpose

Above all, God's plan is bigger than our immediate perspective. Your story is part of His grand design. As you yield to His will, He ensures that every joy and trial contributes to His eternal plan. Your life matters in the broader tapestry of His kingdom, and He's weaving every thread into a beautiful masterpiece for His glory.

Prayer

Lord, thank You for working all things together for my good. Help me to trust Your hand, especially when I can't see the full picture. Remind me that You are not only working in me and for me, but also accomplishing Your greater purpose through my life. In Jesus' name, Amen.

Reflection Question

What current situation in your life do you need to surrender to God, trusting that He is still working for your good and His purpose.

Action Question:

How can I serve God today?

_____

_____

_____

_____

Good morning Holy Spirit, will you speak to me today.

Devotional: The Call of the Shepherd

John 10:27 (KJV)

"My sheep hear my voice, and I know them, and they follow me."

#1 Relationship Requires Listening

Jesus, the Good Shepherd, speaks to those who belong to Him. Hearing His voice begins with a posture of attentiveness—setting aside distractions and tuning in to the Holy Spirit. As you listen, you learn His heart, His guidance, and His will. Cultivate a habit of silent prayer, meditating on Scripture, and being still before the Lord so you can recognize His voice when He calls.

#2 Relationship Requires Intimacy

A sheep knows the Shepherd's voice because of the close bond they share. Likewise, our relationship with Christ deepens when we spend time in His presence—worshiping, reading His Word, and praying. Intimacy with Him is where trust is built and love is nurtured. The more you know Jesus, the easier it becomes to follow where He leads.

#3 Relationship Requires Commitment

Hearing and knowing are only part of the equation; following requires commitment. It's a daily decision to obey His leading and to walk in His ways, even when it's challenging. True discipleship means surrendering your own desires and goals in favor of the path He sets before you, trusting that the Good Shepherd always leads His sheep to safety and abundant life.

Good morning Holy Spirit, will you speak to me today.

Devotional: Words That Build

Ephesians 4:29 (KJV)

"Let no corrupt communication proceed out of your mouth, but that which is good to the use of edifying, that it may minister grace unto the hearers."

#1 Your Words Can Be Damaging

Our words hold great power. Careless or harmful speech can wound others, creating lasting pain or division. Before you speak, pause and ask yourself if what you're about to say will harm someone's spirit or tarnish your witness.

#2 Your Words Can Also Build

The same tongue that can break someone down can also build them up. Use your words as tools of encouragement, compassion, and truth. Whether through a kind greeting, a thoughtful compliment, or an empathetic response, you have the power to lift someone's day and reflect God's love.

#3 Your Words Should Always Minister Grace

Ultimately, God calls us to speak words that minister grace. This means offering understanding, forgiveness, and hope in what we say. When your words point others to God's love and mercy, they become a powerful force for good, helping people see the heart of Christ through you.

Prayer

Lord, help me to be mindful of the words I speak today.
Let my tongue be used to encourage, uplift, and reflect
Your grace. Teach me to recognize when my words can
cause harm, and fill my heart with love so that my speech
always ministers life and hope. In Jesus' name, Amen.

Reflection Question

How can you consciously choose words today that edify
others and demonstrate God's grace?

Action Question:

How can I serve God today?

_____

_____

_____

_____

Good morning Holy Spirit, will you speak to me today.

Devotional: The Finisher

Philippians 1:6 (KJV)

"Being confident of this very thing, that he which hath begun a good work in you will perform it until the day of Jesus Christ."

#1 God Started It, He'll Finish It

God never leaves a project halfway done. If He began a good work in you—stirring your heart, transforming your life—He will see it through to completion. Trust that every season, whether easy or challenging, is part of His process. You might not see the end result yet, but rest assured, He is faithful to finish what He started.

#2 Confidence Is a Finisher

Our role is to walk in confidence. Not in ourselves, but in the One who called us. Confidence propels you forward when doubts arise, reminding you that God's power and purpose are at work. As you trust in His plan, your faith aligns with His promise to bring you to a fulfilled and fruitful end.

#3 He'll Do It in You and Through You

God's work in you isn't just for your benefit—it's also for His glory and for blessing others. As He shapes and refines you, He's simultaneously equipping you to serve, encourage, and inspire those around you. Let Him work in you and watch how He works through you to make a lasting impact in the world.

Prayer

Lord, thank You for beginning a good work in my life. I place my confidence in Your faithfulness and power, trusting You to see this work through to completion. Use me as You transform me, so that I may honor You and bless others. In Jesus' name, Amen.

Reflection Question

In what areas of your life do you need to trust God to finish the work He has started, and how can you walk in confidence today?

Action Question:

How can I serve God today?

_____

_____

_____

_____

Good morning Holy Spirit, will you speak to me today.

Devotional: God's Prevailing Presence

"Then he answered and spake unto me, saying, This is the word of the LORD unto Zerubbabel, saying,

Zechariah 4:6 (KJV)

Not by might, nor by power, but by my spirit, saith the LORD of hosts."

#1 God Will Answer When You Call

When you reach out to God in prayer, He hears you. Like Zerubbabel, you may feel overwhelmed by the challenges before you, but remember that the Lord listens and responds in His perfect timing. Don't hesitate to call upon Him, knowing He's faithful to answer.

#2 God Will Answer with Power

God's answers aren't confined to human strength or resources. What He sets in motion is driven by His Spirit, which surpasses all limitations. Whatever obstacles stand in your way, trust that His power at work in you is greater than any opposition you face.

#3 God's Presence Will Prevail

Ultimately, it's the Lord's presence—His Holy Spirit—that wins the battle. It's not about your might or ability; it's about His sovereign move in your life. When you rely on Him, you'll see His hand prevail in ways you never could accomplish on your own.

Prayer

Lord, thank You for hearing me when I call and for responding with the power of Your Holy Spirit. Teach me to rely on Your presence, trusting that You will prevail in every circumstance. Strengthen my faith and remind me daily that victory is found in You alone. In Jesus' name, Amen.

Reflection Question

Where in your life do you need to stop relying on your own strength and start trusting the Holy Spirit to bring victory?

Action Question:

How can I serve God today?

_____

_____

_____

_____

Good morning Holy Spirit, will you speak to me today.

Devotional: A Fountain of Life

Proverbs 14:27 (KJV)

"The fear of the LORD is a fountain of life, to depart from the snares of death."

#1 Fearing God Is Life

When Scripture speaks of the "fear of the Lord," it's not talking about terror or dread. Instead, it refers to a deep reverence, respect, and awe for who God is. This posture of honor and humility toward Him becomes a constant source of spiritual vitality. Like a fountain that never runs dry, the fear of the Lord pours life into our hearts and minds, refreshing us daily with wisdom and hope.

#2 Fearing God Is Protection in Life

Revering God also acts as a safeguard against life's traps. When we keep Him at the forefront of our decisions, we avoid the snares that can lead us astray. His guidance becomes our compass, steering us away from destructive paths and anchoring us in His truth. By honoring God above all else, we find a protective boundary that keeps us in alignment with His best for our lives.

Prayer

Lord, teach me to reverence You in every area of my life. Help me to remember that true life and protection are found in honoring You. Give me the wisdom to walk in Your ways so I can avoid the snares of life and experience the abundant life You offer. In Jesus' name, Amen.

Reflection Question

How can you cultivate a deeper reverence for God today, allowing His wisdom and protection to guide your every step?

Action Question:

How can I serve God today?

_____

_____

_____

_____

Good morning Holy Spirit, will you speak to me today.

Devotional: Trusting God in Every Detail

Proverbs 3:6 (KJV)

"In all thy ways acknowledge him, and he shall direct thy paths."

#1 See Him in Everything

God is present in every moment of your life—whether big or small, joyful or difficult. Learning to see Him in everything means training your heart to recognize His hand at work all around you. Take a moment to pause and notice where He might be speaking or moving in your everyday routines.

#2 Talk to Him About Anything

God invites you into constant, open communication. There's nothing too small or too big for Him. Sharing your concerns, dreams, fears, and praises with God deepens your relationship and helps you rely on Him more fully. The more you talk with Him, the more you learn to trust His responses.

#3 Trust Him in All Things

Trust grows when we put our faith into practice, especially in uncertain situations. When you acknowledge God in every area—finances, relationships, decisions—He promises to direct your paths. No matter what comes your way, place your confidence in His character and love for you.

Good morning Holy Spirit, will you speak to me today.

Devotional: Trusting His Voice

Proverbs 3:5 (KJV)

"Trust in the LORD with all thine heart; and lean not unto thine own understanding." #1 Trust My Voice

God's voice offers clarity and wisdom beyond our human reasoning. When He speaks, it's not just an opinion—it's truth. To trust His voice means choosing to believe what He says, even when circumstances suggest otherwise. Embrace His words as your solid foundation, rather than relying solely on your own thoughts or emotions.

#2 There's Peace in My Voice

God's voice carries peace. In a world filled with noise and chaos, His guidance brings calmness to an anxious heart. When you sense unrest, pause and listen for His gentle whisper. Allow His reassurance to settle your worries, reminding you that He's in control and His plans for you are good.

#3 My Voice Is Divine Direction

Beyond peace, God's voice provides divine direction for your life. He knows the path you should take and the steps needed to fulfill your purpose. Trust that He's leading you precisely where you need to go. As you obey, you'll discover the fulfillment, wisdom, and protection that come from walking in step with Him.

Prayer

Lord, help me to trust Your voice above my own understanding. When I am uncertain, let me find peace in Your presence. Guide my steps with Your divine direction so that my life may honor You and reflect Your goodness. In Jesus' name, Amen.

Reflection Question

Where in your life do you need to pause, listen for God's voice, and trust His direction above your own understanding?

Action Question:

How can I serve God today?

_____

_____

_____

_____

Good morning Holy Spirit, will you speak to me today.

Devotional: Spiritual Warfare

2 Corinthians 10:4 (KJV)

"(For the weapons of our warfare are not carnal, but mighty through God to the pulling down of strong holds.)"

#1 Focus on the Real Issue

In life's battles, our true enemy isn't always the people or circumstances we see. Behind the scenes, spiritual forces are at work, seeking to discourage and distract us. Recognize that the real issues often lie in the unseen realm—attitudes, thought patterns, or spiritual oppression. By identifying the core problem, we can use the right strategy to overcome it.

#2 Engage the War in the Spirit

God has given us powerful spiritual weapons—His Word, prayer, and the authority of Jesus' name. These are far more potent than any earthly tool or tactic. When we fight by faith and stand on God's promises, strongholds are dismantled and the enemy's plans are defeated. Victory begins when we choose to rely on God's supernatural resources rather than our own strength.

#3 Expect the Change

Once you've recognized the real issue and engaged in spiritual warfare, anticipate God's intervention. Expect strongholds to fall and transformations to occur. Knowing your weapons are mighty through God should give you confidence that changes will come as you stand firm in faith. Your posture of expectation invites God to move powerfully in your situation.

Prayer

Lord, open my eyes to the spiritual realities around me and help me to focus on the true issues I face. Teach me to use the weapons You have provided—Your Word, prayer, and the power of Jesus' name. I expect to see strongholds fall as I trust in You. In Jesus' name, Amen.

Reflection Question

What spiritual battles are you facing today, and how can you apply God's mighty weapons to see real change and breakthrough?

Action Question:

How can I serve God today?

_____

_____

_____

_____

Good morning Holy Spirit, will you speak to me today.

Devotional: Safe in His Name

Proverbs 18:10 (KJV)

"The name of the LORD is a strong tower: the righteous runneth into it, and is safe."

#1 Know His Name

God's name isn't just a label—it represents His character, power, and faithfulness. When you truly know the Lord's name, you recognize Him as the One who saves, heals, and redeems. Spend time in His Word to learn who He is—your Provider, Protector, and Peace.

#2 Know When to Run

Life's challenges can come unexpectedly, and sometimes we try to face them alone. But God invites us to run to Him rather than rely on our own strength. Whether you're overwhelmed by fear, burdened by anxiety, or simply in need of guidance, don't hesitate to call on His name and draw near. In His presence, there's refuge and rest.

#3 Know That There Is Safety

God's name is your fortress—a strong tower that offers unshakable security. In Him, you find protection from the storms of life. Even when circumstances seem uncertain or hostile, remember that you are safe in the shadow of His Almighty presence. Trust that the One who holds you will not fail you.

Prayer

Lord, thank You for being my strong tower. Help me to know You more deeply, to run to You first when trouble comes, and to rest in the safety only You can provide. Teach me to trust in Your name above all else. In Jesus' name, Amen.

Reflection Question

How can you deepen your understanding of God's name today, and what practical steps will you take to run to Him when challenges arise?

Action Question:

How can I serve God today?

_____

_____

_____

_____

Good morning Holy Spirit, will you speak to me today.

Devotional: Love Demonstrated

1 John 4:10–11 (KJV)

"Herein is love, not that we loved God, but that he loved us, and sent his Son to be the propitiation for our sins. Beloved, if God so loved us, we ought also to love one another."

#1 God Demonstrated His Love

God's love is not merely a concept; it's an action He initiated. He sent Jesus—His own Son—to be the propitiation for our sins. This selfless act shows that true love goes beyond words or feelings. God loved us first, and His love is unfailing, unearned, and unmeasured.

#2 His Demonstration Is Our Example

By sending Jesus, God set the ultimate standard for love. We're called to follow this example—an example that costs something, that serves others, and that puts another's well-being above our own. As we look at Jesus' sacrifice, we learn that love is not passive but active, giving, and intentional.

#3 His Love Is Demonstrated Through Us

God's intention is that His love doesn't stop at us but flows through us to others. Because He first loved us, we can now love one another. Our words, attitudes, and acts of service become tangible expressions of God's heart. When we love, we reflect His nature and make Him known to a world that desperately needs Him.

Prayer

Lord, thank You for the overwhelming love You demonstrated by sending Jesus to save me. Teach me to love others the way You've loved me. May my actions, words, and heart reflect Your selfless and boundless love to everyone around me. In Jesus' name, Amen.

Reflection Question

How can you practically demonstrate God's love today, following His example of sacrificial care for others?

Action Question:

How can I serve God today?

_____

_____

_____

_____

Good morning Holy Spirit, will you speak to me today.

Devotional: Confident in Prayer

1 John 5:14 (KJV)

"And this is the confidence that we have in him, that, if we ask anything according to his will, he heareth us."

#1 Prayer Is the Result of Confidence

When you know who God is and believe in His character, you naturally come to Him in prayer. Confidence in God's goodness, power, and love fuels your desire to reach out to Him. Because you know He is trustworthy, prayer becomes more than a ritual—it becomes a genuine conversation with your Heavenly Father.

#2 Confidence Is the Result of Past Prayers

Our confidence in God often grows from seeing how He has answered prayers before. Reflect on moments when He came through—providing, healing, guiding. Each time God answers, your faith becomes stronger, and your assurance in His faithfulness grows, empowering you to pray even more boldly.

#3 Answered Prayer Is Because He Hears Us

We don't serve a distant or indifferent God. When we ask according to His will, He hears us—and His hearing leads to action. Remember that "hearing" in Scripture is an active term; it means God not only listens but also responds. So pray in alignment with His heart, and trust that your petitions have reached His ears.

Good morning Holy Spirit, will you speak to me today.

Devotional: Walking in Authority

Luke 10:19 (KJV)

"Behold, I give unto you power to tread on serpents and scorpions, and over all the power of the enemy: and nothing shall by any means hurt you."

#1 You Have Authority Over the Enemy

Jesus has given you the right to stand firm against every spiritual attack. This authority isn't based on your own strength or merit—it's granted by Christ Himself. Remember, you are not powerless; you are equipped to overcome darkness because of the One who lives in you.

#2 This Authority Is Specifically to Stop the Enemy in Your Life

God's power at work in you is meant to protect and preserve you from harm. As a believer, you can tread on every scheme the enemy tries to bring. Rather than fearing the enemy's tactics, rest in the knowledge that Jesus has already disarmed the powers of darkness on your behalf.

#3 You Must Use This Authority

Having authority doesn't help if we never exercise it. We must speak in faith, stand on God's promises, and pray with boldness. When doubts and trials arise, remember your position in Christ and confidently resist the enemy. Actively use the spiritual weapons God has provided—His Word, prayer, and the name of Jesus—to maintain victory day by day.

Prayer

Lord, thank You for granting me authority over the power of the enemy. Help me to remember that in You, I am already victorious. Teach me to walk boldly in the authority You've given, standing against every attack with faith and confidence. In Jesus' name, Amen.

Reflection Question

How can you intentionally use the authority Christ has given you to overcome spiritual challenges and walk in daily victory?

Action Question:

How can I serve God today?

Good morning Holy Spirit, will you speak to me today.

Devotional: First Things First

Matthew 6:33 (KJV)

"But seek ye first the kingdom of God, and his righteousness; and all these things shall be added unto you." #1 Make God Your Priority

When Jesus tells us to "seek first the kingdom of God," He's inviting us to place Him above everything else. Our time, attention, and decisions should all flow from a desire to honor Him. Rather than allowing the demands of life to dictate our focus, choose to put God at the center.

#2 Make His Values Your Values

Seeking God's kingdom involves more than just a quick prayer or weekly church attendance. It means aligning your heart with His ways. Let His righteousness shape your decisions, your relationships, and even your ambitions. As you adopt His values of love, generosity, purity, and faithfulness, you'll find your life steadily transforming.

#3 Then You Become His Priority

God promises that when we put Him first, He takes care of our needs. "All these things" refers to the everyday provisions and blessings we often worry about. By focusing on His kingdom and His righteousness, we invite His favor and protection. As we make God our priority, He lovingly and faithfully makes us His own.

Prayer

Lord, help me to put You first in everything I do. Teach me to love what You love and value what You value. I trust that as I seek Your kingdom and Your righteousness, You will meet my needs and guide my path. In Jesus' name, Amen.

Reflection Question

What changes can you make today to ensure you're seeking God and His righteousness above all else?

Action Question:

How can I serve God today?

_____

_____

_____

_____

Good morning Holy Spirit, will you speak to me today.

Devotional: Growing Through Grace

1 Peter 5:10 (KJV)

"But the God of all grace, who hath called us unto his eternal glory by Christ Jesus, after that ye have suffered a while, make you perfect, stablish, strengthen, settle you."

#1 God's Grace Is on Your Life

Our God is the "God of all grace." That means no matter what you face—troubles, heartaches, or uncertainties—His grace covers you completely. He is actively pouring out His unmerited favor and strength upon you, equipping you for every challenge.

#2 What You're Going Through Won't Take You Out

Suffering, though difficult, is never final for the believer. The trials you endure won't defeat you because God is with you in the midst of them. He promises that after a season of hardship, He Himself will restore and establish you. Trust that your trials are temporary, but His presence is permanent.

#3 In Fact, You'll Come Out Better

God doesn't just bring you through trials—He refines you in them. He perfects your character, stabilizes your faith, strengthens your resolve, and ultimately settles you on a firm foundation. You emerge from adversity more confident in His power and love, reflecting the growth He's worked within you.

Prayer

Lord, thank You for Your sustaining grace in every season of my life. Remind me that no challenge or trial can overpower Your purposes for me. Strengthen my faith, refine my character, and help me trust that I will come out better, perfectly settled in Your hands. In Jesus' name, Amen.

Reflection Question

How can you lean on God's grace in the middle of your current trials, trusting that you'll emerge stronger and more secure in Him?

Action Question:

How can I serve God today?

_____

_____

_____

_____

Good morning Holy Spirit, will you speak to me today.

Devotional: Living as an Overcomer

John 16:33 (KJV)

"These things I have spoken unto you, that in me ye might have peace. In the world ye shall have tribulation: but be of good cheer; I have overcome the world."

#1 Overcomers Hear God's Voice

Jesus spoke these words so we would know and recognize His truth. Overcomers pay attention to God's voice, allowing His Word to guide their decisions and shape their perspective. When you listen closely to Him—through Scripture, prayer, and the Holy Spirit—you're equipped to stand strong in a world full of tribulation.

#2 Overcomers Walk in God's Peace

Christ's victory enables you to have peace even in the midst of trouble. This peace isn't from your circumstances; it's from the presence of Jesus Himself. Overcomers let God's peace guard their hearts and minds, trusting that He is bigger than any challenge they face.

#3 Overcomers Walk as Overcomers

It's one thing to know you have victory; it's another to live it out daily. Because Jesus has overcome, you can step forward with faith and hope, no matter what comes your way. Overcomers move boldly, confident in the truth that they share in Christ's triumph.

Prayer

Lord, thank You for speaking truth into my life and giving me peace in a troubled world. Teach me to recognize Your voice, rest in Your peace, and walk as an overcomer each day. Remind me that my victory is secure in You. In Jesus' name, Amen.

Reflection Question

In what specific way can you lean on God's voice and peace today to live as an overcomer in your current circumstances?

Action Question:

How can I serve God today?

_____

_____

_____

_____

Good morning Holy Spirit, will you speak to me today.

Devotional: Ask, Believe, Receive

Matthew 21:22 (KJV)

"And all things, whatsoever ye shall ask in prayer, believing, ye shall receive."

#1 Be Specific When You Pray

God invites us to bring all our requests to Him, no matter how large or small. Being specific in prayer shows faith and trust, as it acknowledges that God cares about every detail of our lives. Don't hesitate to name your needs clearly before the Lord; He's ready and willing to hear.

#2 See What You Pray For

Visualizing the answer to your prayer builds expectation. When you pray, imagine God moving on your behalf. This isn't about wishful thinking; it's about aligning your heart with His promises. By faith, see God's provision and breakthrough unfolding, and let that vision stir hope within you.

#3 Expect What You Pray For

Faith involves expecting God to fulfill His Word. When Jesus says, "believing, ye shall receive," He's highlighting the importance of genuine trust. Don't let doubt or past disappointments rob your hope. Expect God to respond in His perfect timing and way, confident that He delights in blessing His children.

Good morning Holy Spirit, will you speak to me today.

Devotional: Staying Alert

1 Peter 5:8 (KJV)

"Be sober, be vigilant; because your adversary the devil, as a roaring lion, walketh about, seeking whom he may devour." #1 Be Serious About Your Salvation

Salvation is more than just a one-time decision; it's a new way of living under the lordship of Christ. Taking your faith seriously means investing time in Scripture, prayer, and fellowship. As you remain rooted in Jesus, you are better able to stand against the enemy's schemes.

#2 Be Watchful of Your Surroundings

A watchful believer pays attention to what influences their heart and mind. Guard your eyes, ears, and thoughts from negativity and temptation. Be mindful of unhealthy relationships or environments that can weaken your walk with Christ. Vigilance helps you recognize and resist the devil's attempts to ensnare you.

#3 Your Enemy Is Looking to End You

Scripture is clear: the enemy's ultimate goal is to devour and destroy. But remember, he is a defeated foe. Through Christ's victory on the cross, you have the authority to stand firm. Being sober-minded and alert ensures you're prepared to resist him, confident in Christ's power and protection.

Prayer

Lord, keep me sober-minded and watchful. Help me take my salvation seriously, guarding my heart against any trap of the enemy. I trust in Your strength to overcome every attack, knowing that You have already won the victory. In Jesus' name, Amen.

Reflection Question

In what areas of your life do you need to be more watchful to protect yourself from the enemy's influence?

Action Question:

How can I serve God today?

_____

_____

_____

_____

Good morning Holy Spirit, will you speak to me today.

Devotional: Be Still and Know

Psalm 46:10 (KJV)

"Be still, and know that I am God: I will be exalted among the heathen, I will be exalted in the earth."

#1 Wait, He's Moving

Sometimes, our greatest act of faith is to do nothing but wait. When God says, "Be still," He's inviting you to pause your striving and trust His unseen hand at work. Even when your situation seems static or overwhelming, He is actively orchestrating details behind the scenes.

#2 Trust, He's Moving

Being still is more than physical rest; it's an inner posture of trust. As you yield your anxieties, plans, and fears to the Lord, you allow Him to move in ways you cannot. Know that His timing is perfect, and He delights in showing Himself strong on your behalf.

#3 He Can Handle It

No matter the size of your challenge, God is bigger. He will be exalted over every obstacle and opposition. Acknowledging Him as God means releasing control, confident that He can—and will—handle it all. In His presence, you find both peace and assurance.

Prayer

Lord, help me to be still before You. Teach me to wait on Your perfect timing and to trust that You are moving, even when I can't see it. Remind me daily that You are

God and can handle every concern in my life. In Jesus' name, Amen.

Reflection Question

What situation do you need to surrender to God today, choosing stillness and trust instead of worry or striving?

Action Question:

How can I serve God today?

_____

_____

_____

_____

Good morning Holy Spirit, will you speak to me today.

Devotional: The Power of His Word

Proverbs 4:20–22 (KJV)

"My son, attend to my words; incline thine ear unto my sayings. Let them not depart from thine eyes; keep them in the midst of thine heart. For they are life unto those that find them, and health to all their flesh." #1 Give Attention to His Word

God urges us to focus on His words. This doesn't mean a casual glance; it's an intentional effort to study, meditate, and truly understand what He's saying. By prioritizing Scripture, we open our hearts to divine wisdom, guidance, and transformation.

#2 Keep His Word

Keeping God's Word goes beyond memorizing verses—it means letting His truths shape your actions and decisions. When you internalize His instructions, they become the compass that guides your choices, helping you align your life with His will.

#3 His Word Gives Life

God's Word is not just information; it brings life and healing to those who receive it. As you dwell on His promises, hope springs up, faith is strengthened, and your spiritual (and often physical) well-being flourishes. His Word is alive and active, capable of bringing renewed purpose and vitality to every area of your life.

Prayer

Lord, thank You for the life and health found in Your Word. Help me to give You my full attention, to guard Your truth in my heart, and to walk in the life-giving power of Scripture every day. In Jesus' name, Amen.

Reflection Question

How can you more intentionally focus on God's Word this week so that it shapes your thoughts, decisions, and overall well-being?

Action Question:

How can I serve God today?

_____

_____

_____

_____

Good morning Holy Spirit, will you speak to me today.

Devotional: The Source of Our Supply

Philippians 4:19 (KJV)

"But my God shall supply all your needs according to his riches in glory by Christ Jesus."

#1 Know Your Source

It's easy to look to our jobs, relationships, or even our own abilities as our primary providers. But Scripture reminds us that God Himself is our true source of every blessing. Recognizing Him as the One who meets our needs frees us from relying on limited resources and helps us focus on His unlimited supply.

#2 Trust Your Source

Knowing that God is your source is one thing; trusting Him is another. When challenges arise—bills stack up or plans fall through—lean on the truth that He's faithful to provide. Trusting your Source means surrendering anxiety and replacing it with faith, confident that God cares for you more than you can imagine.

#3 He's the Source of All You Need

God's supply isn't restricted to material things. He meets emotional, relational, and spiritual needs as well. Whether it's peace in a storm, wisdom for a decision, or comfort in grief, He has a limitless storehouse. Because He is rich in glory, you can count on Him to provide exactly what you need when you need it most.

Prayer

Lord, thank You for being the ultimate source of everything I need. Help me to recognize and trust You in every situation. Remind me that Your riches in glory never run out and that You delight in caring for me. In Jesus' name, Amen.

Reflection Question

Where in your life do you need to shift your trust from earthly resources to God as your true source and provider?

Action Question:

How can I serve God today?

_____

_____

_____

_____

Good morning Holy Spirit, will you speak to me today.

Devotional: God's Temple

1 Corinthians 6:19 (KJV)

"What? know ye not that your body is the temple of the Holy Ghost which is in you, which ye have of God, and ye are not your own?" 1

#1 You Belong to God

When you give your life to Christ, you surrender ownership of yourself to Him. Your identity is now rooted in who He is, and your life is under His loving authority. Recognizing that you belong to God frees you from the pressure of trying to define your own worth, because He has already determined your value and purchased you at a great price.

#2 God Is in You

The Holy Spirit literally resides within you, making your body His temple. This isn't a distant or abstract concept—God is with you and in you. Each moment, His presence offers guidance, comfort, and power to live a life that reflects Him. When you're aware of the Spirit's indwelling presence, it changes how you see yourself and your everyday choices.

#3 What You Do Should Glorify God

Because you belong to Him and He lives in you, the way you live matters. Everything from your words to your actions can either honor or dishonor the God who made you His dwelling place. Whether it's how you treat your body, handle relationships, or carry out your

Prayer

Lord, thank You for speaking to me and calling me by name. Help me to listen to Your voice, deepen my intimacy with You, and commit to following wherever You lead. Teach me to trust You wholeheartedly, knowing You are the Good Shepherd who guides and protects. In Jesus' name, Amen.

Reflection Question

How can you intentionally nurture a deeper listening ear, greater intimacy, and stronger commitment in your relationship with Jesus this week?

Action Question:

How can I serve God today?

_____

_____

_____

_____

Good morning Holy Spirit, will you speak to me today.

Devotional: Fearless

Deuteronomy 31:6 (KJV)

"Be strong and of good courage, fear not, nor be afraid of them: for the LORD thy God, he it is that doth go with thee; he will not fail thee, nor forsake thee."

#1 Walk in Your Strength

God has already equipped you with everything you need to face the challenges ahead. Draw on the strength He has placed in you—your talents, your testimony, and your faith. Stand firm, knowing you're not alone in the battle.

#2 Walk in Courage

Courage isn't the absence of fear; it's moving forward despite it. Let your confidence rest in God's character. He is faithful, and His power is made perfect in your weakness. Take the steps He's calling you to, assured He's with you every step of the way.

#3 Give Them No Energy (Time)

Negativity, doubt, and fear only gain power when we dwell on them. Choose not to invest your time or mental space in the voices that say you can't move forward. Keep your eyes on what God says instead, and trust His promises over any opposition.

#4 God Will Not Fail You

Ultimately, your greatest assurance is God's presence and His promise never to fail or forsake you. Even when circumstances feel overwhelming, He holds you securely in His care. Rest in His unfailing love, and let that love propel you to live boldly.

Prayer

Lord, thank You for walking with me through every challenge and strengthening me with Your power. Help me to face fears with courage, to ignore the distractions of doubt, and to remember that You will never fail me. I trust You wholeheartedly as I walk in the boldness You've provided. In Jesus' name, Amen.

Reflection Question

How can you intentionally focus your energy on God's promises rather than the distractions or fears around you today?

Action Question:

How can I serve God today?

_____

_____

_____

_____

Prayer

Lord, help me to see You at work in every aspect of my life. Remind me to bring everything—my hopes, my worries, my gratitude—directly to You. Increase my faith so that I can trust You in all things, knowing You will faithfully guide my steps. In Jesus' name, Amen.

Reflection Question

Where can you more intentionally acknowledge God in your life today, and how can you practice trusting Him with the details?

Action Question:

How can I serve God today?

_____

_____

_____

_____

Good morning Holy Spirit, will you speak to me today.

Devotional: Arise and Shine

Isaiah 60:1 (KJV)

"Arise, shine; for thy light is come, and the glory of the LORD is risen upon thee." #1 We Are Called to Be Lights

God's people are not meant to hide in the shadows. He calls us to step forward and shine brightly in a dark world. When you accept Christ, you become a beacon of His hope and love. Your life becomes a testimony of His grace, pointing others toward the light of Jesus.

#2 We Are Expected to Shine

Being a light isn't just about receiving God's goodness for ourselves; it's also about reflecting it for others. Whether through acts of service, words of encouragement, or genuine compassion, your everyday choices can radiate God's love. Don't underestimate the impact of your faithful witness.

#3 It's God's Glory That We Release

Ultimately, any light we shine comes from the glory of the Lord within us. As His glory rises upon you, it empowers you to display His character—His kindness, holiness, and truth—to a watching world. When people see the light in you, they are glimpsing the majesty of God Himself.

Prayer

Lord, thank You for calling me to be a light in this world. Help me to live boldly, shining Your love and truth wherever I go. May my life reflect Your glory so that others are drawn to You. In Jesus' name, Amen.

Reflection Question

In what practical ways can you shine God's light today so that others experience His glory through you?

Action Question:

How can I serve God today?

_____

_____

_____

_____

Prayer

Lord, thank You for the confidence I can have in bringing my requests before You. Strengthen my faith through the memories of past answered prayers. As I pray according to Your will, remind me that You hear me and are ready to respond. In Jesus' name, Amen.

Reflection Question

What past answered prayers can you recall today that will boost your confidence to pray more boldly in the present?

Action Question:

How can I serve God today?

Good morning Holy Spirit, will you speak to me today.

Devotional: Stepping Out in Faith

Hebrews 11:8 (KJV)

"By faith Abraham, when he was called to go out into a place which he should after receive for an inheritance, obeyed; and he went out, not knowing whither he went."
#1 Faith Is Obedience

Abraham didn't just believe God in theory—he took action. True faith compels us to obey even when the outcome isn't fully clear. Like Abraham, we too must act on God's direction, trusting that He knows where He's leading us. Our willingness to follow demonstrates the genuineness of our faith.

#2 Faith Is Dependence

Leaving his home required Abraham to depend entirely on God for guidance, provision, and protection. Faith means leaning on God's promises rather than our own resources. When we depend on Him, we acknowledge that everything—our next step, our future, our very breath—ultimately comes from His hand.

#3 Faith Is "Ignorance"

Abraham truly didn't know where he was going. Faith often requires moving forward without all the details. It's not ignorance of God's character, but a willingness to trust Him despite our limited understanding. We walk by faith, not by sight, confident that the One who calls us knows the way perfectly.

Prayer

Lord, teach me to obey You wholeheartedly, depend on You completely, and trust You even when the path is unclear. Give me the courage to walk in faith like Abraham, knowing You hold my future in Your hands. In Jesus' name, Amen.

Reflection Question

Where in your life is God calling you to step out in faith, even though you don't know all the details? How can you obey and depend on Him today despite the unknowns?

Action Question:

How can I serve God today?

_____

_____

_____

_____

Prayer

Lord, thank You for the privilege of coming to You in prayer. Help me to be specific as I present my needs, to see Your hand at work by faith, and to expect answers according to Your perfect will. I trust in Your goodness and power to provide. In Jesus' name, Amen.

Reflection Question

How can you be more intentional in your prayer life by being specific, visualizing God's provision, and expecting Him to answer?

Action Question:

How can I serve God today?

_____

_____

_____

_____

Good morning Holy Spirit, will you speak to me today.

Devotional: A Life Free in Christ

John 5:18 (KJV)

"We know that whosoever is born of God sinneth not; but he that is begotten of God keepeth himself, and that wicked one toucheth him not." 1 #1 You Are No Longer a Sinner (After Salvation)

Through faith in Christ, you've been set free from the power and penalty of sin. Though believers are not sinless in the sense of never making mistakes, the dominating rule of sin over your life is broken. You are now a new creation, empowered by God's Spirit to live righteously and turn away from old patterns.

#2 You Can Now Walk in Authority

Being born of God grants you spiritual authority. You're not subject to the enemy's schemes as you once were. Instead, you stand firm in Jesus' victory. Through prayer, declaring God's Word, and daily obedience, you exercise the authority Christ has given, resisting sin and the influence of the enemy.

#3 You Are Now Shielded from the Clutches of the Enemy

In Christ, you have divine protection. The "wicked one" cannot claim ownership of your life because you belong to God. This doesn't mean you'll never face trials, but it does mean you can resist fear and temptation, assured of God's safeguarding power.

Prayer

Lord, thank You for the freedom and authority I have in Christ. Remind me daily that sin no longer rules me and that I stand under Your protection. Strengthen me to walk in righteousness, trusting in Your saving power. In Jesus' name, Amen.

Reflection Question

How can you actively exercise your spiritual authority and lean on God's protection in areas where you once felt weak or bound by sin?

Action Question:

How can I serve God today?

---

responsibilities, strive to bring glory to the One who calls you His own.

Prayer

Lord, thank You for making me Your temple. Help me to remember that I belong to You and that You live within me. May my thoughts, words, and actions honor You, reflecting Your presence to those around me. In Jesus' name, Amen.

Reflection Question

What specific changes can you make today to live in a way that honors God, recognizing that your body is His temple?

Action Question:

How can I serve God today?

_____

_____

_____

_____

Good morning Holy Spirit, will you speak to me today.

Devotional: Continual Praise

Psalm 34:1 (KJV)

"I will bless the LORD at all times: his praise shall continually be in my mouth." #1 Make Your Praise Personal

David's commitment to bless the Lord "at all times" stems from a personal relationship with God. When your praise is personal, it's rooted in gratitude for who He is to you—your Savior, your Provider, your Comforter. Reflect on the specific ways God has been faithful and let your personal encounters with Him fuel your worship.

#2 Make Your Praise Persistent

Praising God continually is a choice, not a feeling. Whether you're experiencing the heights of joy or the depths of struggle, make praise your constant posture. Persistence in praise shifts your focus from problems to the One who has the power to solve them. Consistency in worship aligns your heart with God's truth, regardless of life's circumstances.

#3 Watch Your Praise Release Your Power

Praise isn't just an act of adoration; it's also a spiritual weapon. As you lift God high, you invite His presence and authority into your situation. Praising God in the midst of life's challenges can break chains, bring peace, and ignite hope. When praise goes up, God's power goes to work in and around you.

Prayer

Lord, thank You for being worthy of my continual praise. Help me make my worship personal, persistent, and powerful. Teach me to bless You at all times, trusting that my praise ushers in Your presence and releases divine strength in my life. In Jesus' name, Amen.

Reflection Question

In what specific way can you practice continual praise today, regardless of your current circumstances?

Action Question:

How can I serve God today?

_____

_____

_____

_____

Good morning Holy Spirit, will you speak to me today.

Devotional: Daily Benefits

Psalms 68:19(KJV)

"Blessed be the Lord, who daily loadeth us with benefits, even the God of our salvation. Selah."

#1 We Bless the Lord

Worship begins with honoring God for who He is. By declaring "Blessed be the Lord," we acknowledge His sovereignty and goodness. Setting our hearts and voices toward praise aligns us with heaven's perspective, reminding us that He is worthy of all glory.

#2 He Blesses Us

God doesn't just bless occasionally—He "daily loadeth us with benefits." His generous heart pours out favor, provision, and protection. Each new day offers opportunities to witness His grace in action. Whether we notice it or not, God consistently showers our lives with gifts both big and small.

#3 We Benefit from It All

Everything we receive flows from the God of our salvation. We benefit spiritually, emotionally, and physically because of His faithful love. As we draw near to Him in gratitude, our hearts become more aware of His constant care, creating even deeper wells of thankfulness and joy.

Prayer

Lord, I bless Your name today and thank You for daily loading my life with benefits. Open my eyes to see Your hand in all things and to appreciate every good gift You provide. Let my heart overflow with gratitude as I trust in Your unending love and salvation. In Jesus' name, Amen.

Reflection Question

How can you become more aware of God's daily blessings in your life, and how will you express your gratitude to Him today?

Action Question:

How can I serve God today?

_____

_____

_____

_____

Good morning Holy Spirit, will you speak to me today.

Devotional: You Are the Light

Matthew 5:16 (KJV)

"Let your light so shine before men, that they may see your good works, and glorify your Father which is in heaven."

#1 Let It Shine

You carry the light of Jesus within you. Don't hide it or hesitate to share it with others. Whether through acts of kindness, encouraging words, or simply being present for someone in need, let the love of Christ radiate from your life.

#2 Let Them See It Shine

Your light isn't just for you—it's for those around you. When your good works point others to God's grace, it stirs hope and curiosity in their hearts. People should be able to look at how you live and see a reflection of Christ's character and compassion.

#3 Then He Will Shine

Ultimately, your light leads back to the Father. As you serve, care, and love in Jesus' name, God is glorified. Your life becomes a testimony that draws people closer to Him. When you let your light shine, He shines through you, making His presence known to a watching world.

Prayer

Lord, help me to let Your light shine through my words and actions. Keep me mindful that everything I do can lead others to know You better. May my life radiate Your love and cause others to glorify You. In Jesus' name, Amen.

Reflection Question

How can you intentionally let the light of Christ shine through you today, pointing others to God's love and grace?

Action Question:

How can I serve God today?

_____

_____

_____

_____

Good morning Holy Spirit, will you speak to me today.

Devotional: Replacing Worry with Peace

Philippians 4:6–7 (KJV)

"Be careful for nothing; but in every thing by prayer and supplication with thanksgiving let your requests be made known unto God. And the peace of God, which passeth all understanding, shall keep your hearts and minds through Christ Jesus." #1 Worry Is Not an Option

Life presents countless reasons to worry—financial struggles, health issues, relationship concerns. Yet God's command is clear: "Be careful for nothing," meaning we should be anxious for nothing. When you feel worry creeping in, remember that it's not your God-given response. Instead of letting anxiety rule your heart, choose to reject it and lean on God's faithfulness.

#2 Everything Requires Prayer

Big or small, every concern belongs at the feet of Jesus. If it matters to you, it matters to Him. Rather than turning to worry, turn to prayer. In every circumstance, let your requests be heard by the One who loves you unconditionally and has the power to act. Consistency in prayer transforms your perspective, building faith and hope.

#3 Prayer Over Worry Equals Peace

When you replace worry with prayer, gratitude, and trust, God promises "the peace of God, which passeth all understanding." This peace isn't rooted in your circumstances; it's rooted in the presence and power of Christ. As you pray, your heart finds rest, and your mind experiences calm in the midst of life's challenges.

Prayer

Lord, thank You for inviting me to bring all my worries and requests to You. Help me to remember that worry is not my portion; prayer is. As I place my concerns in Your hands, fill me with Your peace that surpasses all understanding. Strengthen me to trust You more each day. In Jesus' name, Amen.

Reflection Question

Which worries are you holding onto today, and how can you turn each one into a prayer that invites God's peace into your heart?

Action Question:

How can I serve God today?

_____

_____

_____

_____

Good morning Holy Spirit, will you speak to me today.

Devotional: Serving God by Serving Others

Matthew 25:40 (KJV)

"And the King shall answer and say unto them, Verily I say unto you, Inasmuch as ye have done it unto one of the least of these my brethren, ye have done it unto me." #1 God Expects Us to Serve Others

From the very beginning, Scripture points to God's heart for compassion and generosity. He calls us to be His hands and feet in a world filled with need. Serving others isn't just a suggestion; it's part of our purpose as followers of Christ. Whether it's meeting someone's physical, emotional, or spiritual need, each act of service reveals God's love in a tangible way.

#2 Serving Others Is a Sign of Our Relationship with God

Jesus taught that we can measure our love for Him by the way we treat people in need. Genuine service to others—especially those who are marginalized or hurting—reflects a heart aligned with God's heart. It demonstrates that our faith isn't just words but is alive and active, shaped by Christ's example of love and humility.

#3 When We Serve Others, We Serve God

The remarkable promise in Matthew 25:40 is that every act of kindness done for "the least of these" is counted as if done directly unto Christ Himself. This truth transforms the way we see people and opportunities to help. Serving isn't a chore or burden; it's an opportunity to worship God through compassionate action. In caring for others, we care for Him.

Prayer

Lord, thank You for the reminder that serving others is serving You. Open my eyes to the needs around me and give me a compassionate heart to respond. Help me to love and serve with humility, remembering that every act of service honors You. In Jesus' name, Amen.

Reflection Question

What practical step can you take today to serve someone in need, recognizing that in doing so, you are serving God Himself?

Action Question:

How can I serve God today?

_____

_____

_____

_____

Good morning Holy Spirit, will you speak to me today.

Devotional: Life in the Spirit

John 6:63 (KJV)

"It is the spirit that quickeneth; the flesh profiteth nothing: the words that I speak unto you, they are spirit, and they are life."

#1 Living in the Spirit Gives Life

Jesus reminds us that true, life-giving power comes from the Spirit, not from our own human effort. When we rely on the Holy Spirit, we experience real transformation—our hearts are renewed, our minds are sharpened, and our souls find true rest in God.

#2 There's No Profit in the Flesh

Our human strength, talents, and resources can't produce eternal results on their own. Without the Spirit, our efforts fall short. Recognize the limitations of purely human endeavors and remember that genuine, lasting fruit comes from allowing God's Spirit to work through you.

#3 The Source of the Spirit Is God's Word

Jesus' words are "spirit" and "life." Scripture isn't just information—it is divinely inspired truth that fuels our spirits. By immersing ourselves in God's Word, we invite the Holy Spirit to shape our thoughts, guide our actions, and fill our hearts with life-giving power.

Prayer

Lord, thank You for the life-giving power of Your Spirit and Your Word. Teach me to depend on You rather than my own strength. Let Your Word permeate my heart so that everything I do flows from the power of Your Spirit. In Jesus' name, Amen.

Reflection Question

In what specific ways can you rely more on the Holy Spirit and God's Word instead of your own strength or abilities this week?

Action Question:

How can I serve God today?

_____

_____

_____

_____

Good morning Holy Spirit, will you speak to me today.

Devotional: Cultivating a Heart of Kindness

Ephesians 4:31,32 (KJV)

"Let all bitterness, and wrath, and anger, and clamour, and evil speaking, be put away from you, with all malice." 32 And be ye kind one to another, tenderhearted, forgiving one another, even as God for Christ's sake hath forgiven you.

#1 Don't Be Consumed by Anger, Wrath, and Malice

Bitterness and anger can creep into our hearts, poisoning our thoughts and attitudes. When we hold onto these negative emotions, they begin to consume us, clouding our judgment and hindering our ability to love others well. Recognize these feelings for what they are—destructive influences that God calls us to release.

#2 What You Are Consumed With, You Will Act On

Our actions flow from whatever fills our hearts. If anger or resentment takes root, it will eventually show up in our words and behaviors. Conversely, if we allow God's love and peace to dwell within us, our actions will reflect grace and compassion. Pay attention to what occupies your mind, and choose what you allow to shape your responses.

#3 Kindness Is Key

Ephesians 4:32 (the next verse) reminds us to be kind and tenderhearted, forgiving one another. Kindness has the power to disarm hostility and soften hardened hearts—both ours and others'. Even the simplest act of kindness can be a profound demonstration of God's character to those around you.

#4 Forgiveness Is God

The ability to forgive comes from recognizing how much we have been forgiven by God. When we extend forgiveness, we mirror the grace that God has shown us through Jesus Christ. Forgiveness isn't about excusing harmful behavior; it's about choosing to release resentment and entrust justice to God. In doing so, we walk in freedom and display His love.

Prayer

Lord, help me to let go of bitterness, anger, and malice in every form. Fill my heart with Your love so that I act in kindness and extend forgiveness to others. Thank You for the grace You've shown me; teach me to share that grace freely. In Jesus' name, Amen.

Reflection Question

What negative emotions or attitudes do you need to release today so that you can show kindness and forgiveness to those around you?

Action Question:

How can I serve God today?

_____

_____

_____

_____

Good morning Holy Spirit, will you speak to me today.

Devotional: Genuine Love and Goodness

Romans 12:9 (KJV)

"Let love be without dissimulation. Abhor that which is evil; cleave to that which is good." #1 Love Purely

God calls us to love sincerely—free from hidden agendas or pretenses. True love doesn't seek personal gain; it puts the wellbeing of others first. Examine your heart and motives when extending kindness. Is your care rooted in selfless compassion, or are you seeking something in return? As you love purely, you reflect the genuine, sacrificial love God shows us.

#2 Run from Evil

"Abhor" is a strong word that means to hate or turn away from something. We're to run from anything that draws us away from God's righteousness—be it thoughts, habits, or environments that stir up sin in our hearts. This doesn't mean avoiding people who struggle, but rather rejecting the sin itself, standing firm in holiness and integrity.

#3 Chase What's Good

Rather than only avoiding evil, Scripture instructs us to actively cleave (hold fast) to what is good. Seek out what is pure, helpful, and uplifting. Whether it's nourishing your mind with God's Word, surrounding yourself with encouraging community, or engaging in acts of service, make goodness your pursuit. When you do, you'll experience deeper joy and an increased awareness of God's presence.

Prayer

Lord, help me to love others sincerely, just as You have loved me. Give me the wisdom to recognize and reject what is evil, and the passion to cling to all that is good. May my life reflect Your holiness, grace, and compassion. In Jesus' name, Amen.

Reflection Question

In what practical ways can you "run from evil" and "chase what's good" in your daily life, ensuring that your love remains pure and Christ-centered?

Action Question:

How can I serve God today?

_____

_____

_____

_____

Good morning Holy Spirit, will you speak to me today.

Devotional: Living, Moving, and Thriving in Him

Acts 17:28 (KJV)

"For in him we live, and move, and have our being; as certain also of your own poets have said, For we are also his offspring." #1 We Live in Him

Our very existence is grounded in God. Everything—from our first breath to our daily sustenance—originates with Him. Recognizing that our life is a gift from the Creator helps us remain humble and thankful. Every moment is an opportunity to acknowledge His sustaining power and grace.

#2 We Move in Him

Each step we take, each plan we make, we do so under His watchful care. God is not a distant observer; He is actively involved in our everyday movements. When we remember this truth, it changes how we approach our day-to-day tasks, filling us with purpose and reminding us to rely on His guidance.

#3 We Thrive in Him

To "have our being" in God means we find true fulfillment and purpose in His presence. We don't just survive; we flourish when rooted in Him. Whether it's spiritual growth, meaningful relationships, or fulfilling dreams, all genuine thriving comes from staying connected to the Source of life.

Prayer

Lord, thank You for being my source of life, my guide, and the One in whom I truly thrive. Help me to live with constant gratitude, to walk in humble dependence, and to seek Your presence in all that I do. In Jesus' name, Amen.

Reflection Question

What practical steps can you take today to remain mindful that you live, move, and thrive in the presence of God?

Action Question:

How can I serve God today?

_____

_____

_____

_____

Good morning Holy Spirit, will you speak to me today.

Devotional: Fearless in God

2 Timothy 1:7 (KJV)

"For God hath not given us the spirit of fear; but of power, and of love, and of a sound mind."

1. We Are Not Afraid

Fear does not come from God. Whenever anxiety or doubt creeps in, remember that the Lord has already equipped you with courage. Place your trust in Him, and let His Word remind you that fear has no claim on your life.

2. We Have the Power

God's gift to us includes divine power—not human strength that fails, but a heavenly force that energizes us to overcome challenges. Draw on His power through prayer, faith, and active obedience, confident that you're never walking alone.

3. We Have the Love

Love isn't just an emotion; it's a powerful force that reflects God's heart. This love fuels compassion, humility, and unity. As you tap into His love, you not only minister to others but also grow stronger in faith and resilience.

4. We're Ready to Move

Armed with power, love, and a sound mind, you're prepared to take steps of bold faith. Fear no longer holds you back; instead, it propels you to rely on God's promises. Move forward with confidence, trusting the One who called you.

Prayer

Lord, thank You for replacing my fears with courage, equipping me with power, love, and a sound mind. Help me to move forward in faith, knowing that You are with me every step of the way. In Jesus' name, Amen.

Reflection Question

Where in your life can you replace fear with faith, stepping out boldly in God's power and

love?

Action Question:

How can I serve God today?

_____

_____

_____

_____

Good morning Holy Spirit, will you speak to me today.

Devotional: Embracing the New Thing

Isaiah 43:18–19 (KJV)

"Remember ye not the former things, neither consider the things of old. Behold, I will do a new thing; now it shall spring forth; shall ye not know it? I will even make a way in the wilderness, and rivers in the desert."

1. Don't Expect the New to Look Like the Old

God's plans often exceed our expectations. When He promises something new, it won't simply be an upgraded version of the past—it will be entirely different. Sometimes, clinging to old experiences or comfort zones can blind us to the fresh ways God wants to move. Be open to His unfolding work, even if it doesn't resemble what you've known before.

2. Expect New and Greater

The Lord doesn't merely give replacements; He offers upgrades that bring deeper purpose and blessing. Anticipate God's best in your life. By faith, look forward to greater joy, peace, and fruitfulness. Believe that the "new thing" He's working on will surpass anything you've seen before, because His resources and creativity are limitless.

3. God Will Make a Way Out of No Way

In the midst of life's deserts, God promises living water. When you can't see a path forward, He creates one. Even if you're navigating a season of dryness or uncertainty, trust that He's the God who transforms wilderness places into abundant spaces. His power is made evident when all other options seem impossible.

Prayer

Lord, thank You for the promise of something new and greater. Help me release the old so I can embrace Your fresh work in my life. When situations appear hopeless, remind me that You are the God who makes a way where there seems to be none. In Jesus' name, Amen.

Reflection Question

What old patterns or expectations do you need to let go of so you can fully receive and recognize the "new thing" God is doing in your life?

Action Question:

How can I serve God today?

_____

_____

_____

_____

Good morning Holy Spirit, will you speak to me today.

Devotional: The Unstoppable Word

Isaiah 55:11 (KJV)

"So shall my word be that goeth forth out of my mouth: it shall not return unto me void, but it shall accomplish that which I please, and it shall prosper in the thing whereto I sent it." 1. The Word Has Purpose

God's Word isn't random or idle; it carries intentional purpose. Every promise, instruction, and prophecy is sent with a divine agenda. When we read and meditate on Scripture, we tap into God's eternal plan. Be confident that when you apply His Word to your life, it will lead you toward His intended outcome.

2. The Word Has Power

Because it originates from God, His Word comes with unmatched authority and effectiveness. It's not bound by time or circumstance. When you stand on a promise from God's Word, you're standing on something unshakable. Whether it's comfort in grief, guidance in confusion, or strength in weakness, the power of His Word can transform any situation.

3. The Word Will Prosper You

Not only does God's Word accomplish His will—it also brings prosperity to those who embrace it. This prosperity isn't just about material gain; it's about thriving in every area of life: spiritual, emotional, relational. When you align yourself with the purposes of God, you'll find He provides all you need to succeed according to His perfect plan.

Prayer

Lord, thank You for the life-giving power of Your Word.
Help me to recognize and submit to its purpose in my life.
May Your Word accomplish all You intend, and may I
experience Your abundance as I trust in Your promises.
In Jesus' name, Amen.

Reflection Question

How can you intentionally incorporate God's Word into
your daily routine, trusting its power and purpose to
prosper you in every season?

Action Question:

How can I serve God today?

_____

_____

_____

_____

Good morning Holy Spirit, will you speak to me today.

Devotional: Peace Broker

Romans 12:18 (KJV)

"If it be possible, as much as lieth in you, live peaceably with all men." 1. Believe in the Possibility of Peace

God's Word encourages us to strive for harmony with everyone, reminding us that peace is possible. No matter the tension or difficulty in a relationship, we're called to see each situation through the lens of God's reconciling power. Before you assume conflict is inevitable, remember that through Christ, even strained relationships can find healing and peace.

2. Know and Live What's in You

The Holy Spirit resides within every believer, producing qualities like love, joy, and peace. As a child of God, you have access to supernatural patience, kindness, and self-control. Tapping into these Spirit-given resources helps you approach conflict with grace. When you choose to live from what's already in you—Christ's peace—you set the tone for reconciliation and understanding.

3. Everyone Is a Target for God's Grace

It's easier to show kindness to those who reciprocate, but God's command extends to "all men," including those who challenge us. Viewing others as targets of God's grace transforms the way we interact. Rather than seeing a difficult person as an enemy, consider how God's love might reach them through your patience, forgiveness, or gentle words.

Prayer

Lord, thank You for the gift of Your peace and the power
of Your Spirit at work in me. Help me to believe in the
possibility of peace, to live out the grace You've deposited
within me, and to see others as worthy recipients of Your
love. In Jesus' name, Amen.

Reflection Question

Who in your life could benefit from a peaceful approach
or an extra measure of grace, and how can you practically
extend that peace today?

Action Question:

How can I serve God today?

_____

_____

_____

_____

Good morning Holy Spirit, will you speak to me today.

Devotional: Commit and Be Established

Proverbs 16:3 (KJV)

"Commit thy works unto the LORD, and thy thoughts shall be established."

1. Commit Your Heart to God

True commitmcnt begins on the inside—before your deeds and decisions ever take shape. When you give your heart to God, you surrender your motives, desires, and intentions to Him. As you offer your heart in worship and obedience, He transforms it, aligning your plans with His will.

2. Plan What God Gives You

Once your heart is anchored in God, your plans flow from His leading. Seek His guidance through prayer and Scripture, and allow the Holy Spirit to shape your thoughts and dreams. When you plan under God's direction, you're actively partnering with Him to accomplish His good purposes in your life.

3. God Will Establish His Heart in You

God honors those who commit their works to Him. As you release your ambitions and decisions into His hands, He steadies your mind, clarifies your direction, and strengthens your resolve. In the end, you'll find that the very heart of God becomes your own, and your thoughts become firmly rooted in His eternal perspective.

Prayer

Lord, I commit my heart, my plans, and my work to You today. Guide me in every decision, and let my thoughts be established by Your wisdom and love. Shape my desires so they align with Your will, and help me trust that You will bring them to fulfillment. In Jesus' name, Amen.

Reflection Question

What specific plans or decisions can you commit to the Lord today, trusting Him to establish both your heart and your thoughts?

Action Question:

How can I serve God today?

_____

_____

_____

_____

Good morning Holy Spirit, will you speak to me today.

Devotional: Boldness Through Righteousness

Proverbs 28:1 (KJV)

"The wicked flee when no man pursueth: but the righteous are bold as a lion."

#1 Righteousness Gives Confidence

Righteousness—living in alignment with God's Word—gives you a clear conscience and unshakable confidence. When you know you're walking in God's truth, you have nothing to fear. The assurance that you're right with God allows ?

"If there be therefore any consolation in Christ, if any comfort of love, if any fellowship of the Spirit, if any bowels and mercies, Fulfil ye my joy, that ye be like minded, having the same love, being of one accord, of one mind." #1 Love Like Jesus Loved

Jesus' love is the ultimate standard. It is sacrificial, unconditional, and focused on others. He gave of Himself entirely for our sake, not because we deserved it, but because His love is boundless. To love like Jesus means to put others first, extending grace, forgiveness, and compassion without reservation.

#2 Love Without Motive

True love doesn't seek personal gain or recognition. It is given freely, expecting nothing in return. When we love without hidden agendas, we reflect the heart of Christ and create space for authentic relationships. Love becomes a powerful force for unity when it flows from a place of sincerity and selflessness.

#3 Let It Be About Them and Not You

Genuine love shifts the focus from ourselves to others. Paul reminds us to be like minded and unified in love, making it about the needs, growth, and well-being of others. When we prioritize others over ourselves, we create an atmosphere where God's love is evident, and His joy is fulfilled in us.

Prayer

Lord, thank You for the example of selfless love You've shown through Jesus. Help me to love others without selfish motives, always seeking their good above my own. Unite my heart with others in love and humility, so that we may reflect Your glory together. In Jesus' name, Amen.

Reflection Question

Who can you focus on today, loving them selflessly and reflecting Jesus' love in your actions and attitude?

Action Question:

How can I serve God today?

_____

_____

_____

_____

Good morning Holy Spirit, will you speak to me today.

Devotional: Glory Through the Trouble

2 Corinthians 4:17 (KJV)

"For our light affliction, which is but for a moment, worketh for us a far more exceeding and eternal weight of glory."

1. You Won't Escape All Trouble

Life comes with challenges—afflictions that test your faith and push you to your limits. Even as a believer, trouble is inevitable. But take heart: these difficulties are not a sign of God's absence but an opportunity for His presence to be revealed in new ways.

2. Trouble Won't Outlast You

Paul calls our afflictions "light" and "momentary" in comparison to eternity. While it may not feel light now, your troubles are temporary, and they pale in comparison to the eternal glory awaiting you. God's promises ensure that your trials have an expiration date, but His glory is everlasting.

3. The Trouble Is Working in Your Favor

God doesn't waste your pain. Every challenge you endure is working for you, refining your character, building your faith, and preparing you for something greater. What feels like a setback now is setting you up for an eternal reward far beyond what you can imagine. Trust that God is using your trouble for your good and His glory.

Prayer

Lord, thank You for the reminder that my troubles are temporary and that You are using them for a greater purpose. Help me to trust You through every trial, knowing that each challenge is working in my favor and preparing me for an eternal weight of glory. Strengthen my faith as I wait for Your promises to unfold. In Jesus' name, Amen.

Reflection Question

What current challenge can you view through the lens of God's eternal purpose, trusting that He is working it for your good?

Action Question:

How can I serve God today?

_____

_____

_____

_____

Good morning Holy Spirit, will you speak to me today.

Devotional: The Power of Endurance

Matthew 10:22 (KJV)

"And ye shall be hated of all men for my name's sake: but he that endureth to the end shall be saved." #1 Endurance Is Persevering

Following Christ isn't always easy. Challenges, opposition, and rejection may come because of your faith. Endurance means choosing to press forward despite difficulties, staying true to God's Word and His promises. Perseverance requires spiritual resilience, fueled by trust in the One who has already overcome the world.

#2 Endurance Is to Be Patient

Endurance isn't just about surviving; it's about waiting on God with faith and hope. Patience allows you to trust God's timing and plan, even when the journey feels long or uncertain. As you endure, remember that God is working all things together for good, even in seasons of waiting.

#3 Endurance Is Maintaining His Presence

True endurance comes from abiding in God's presence. When life's challenges arise, staying connected to Him through prayer, worship, and His Word gives you the strength to keep going. His presence provides peace in the storm and the power to endure until the end, knowing salvation is assured.

Prayer

Lord, thank You for the promise of salvation for those who endure. Teach me to persevere through challenges, to be patient in difficult seasons, and to stay rooted in Your presence. Strengthen me daily so I may remain faithful to You, no matter what comes my way. In Jesus' name, Amen.

Reflection Question

What challenges are you currently facing, and how can you lean on God's presence to help you endure with patience and perseverance?

Action Question:

How can I serve God today?

_____

_____

_____

_____

Good morning Holy Spirit, will you speak to me today.

Devotional: Joy in Trials

James 1:2 (KJV)

"My brethren, count it all joy when ye fall into divers temptations." #1 Trials Are Inevitable

Life is filled with challenges, and trials are a part of the journey for every believer. They're not a sign of failure or lack of faith but an opportunity for growth. Accepting that trials will come helps you prepare your heart to face them with grace and trust in God's plan.

#2 Trials Can Come in Packs

James mentions "divers temptations," reminding us that trials often come in clusters, not in isolation. When challenges feel overwhelming, remember that God's strength is greater than the weight of any trial. He's present in every situation, giving you what you need to endure and overcome.

#3 You Control the Impact

While you can't control when or how trials come, you can control how they affect you. Choosing to count it all joy doesn't mean pretending trials aren't difficult—it means trusting that God will use them for your good. Your response determines whether trials strengthen your faith or shake it. Lean on God, and let your joy be rooted in His unchanging faithfulness.

Prayer

Lord, thank You for the reminder that trials are opportunities for growth. Help me to see challenges through the lens of faith, trusting that You are working in every situation. Strengthen me to choose joy, knowing that You are with me and will bring me through. In Jesus' name, Amen.

Reflection Question

How can you shift your perspective today to see trials as opportunities to grow and trust in God's plan?

Action Question:

How can I serve God today?

_____

_____

_____

_____

Good morning Holy Spirit, will you speak to me today.

Devotional: The Power of Belief

Mark 9:23 (KJV)

"Jesus said unto him, If thou canst believe, all things are possible to him that believeth."

#1 Can You Believe?

The question Jesus asks isn't about His power or ability—it's about our faith. The foundation of every miracle and breakthrough is belief. Faith isn't about having all the answers; it's about trusting God's power and promises, even when circumstances seem impossible. Ask yourself today: Do I truly believe God can do what He says?

#2 What's Possible Is What You Believe

Your belief shapes your reality. Jesus says "all things are possible" for those who believe, meaning that the limits we face are often ones we place on ourselves. When you align your faith with God's limitless power, the impossible becomes possible. What you believe opens the door for God to move in extraordinary ways in your life.

Prayer

Lord, help me to believe in Your power and promises without doubt or hesitation. Strengthen my faith so I can trust You fully, even in the face of impossibilities. Teach me to align my thoughts and actions with the truth that all things are possible for those who believe. In Jesus' name, Amen.

Reflection Question

What area of your life needs the faith to believe that "all things are possible," and how can you take a step of trust today?

Action Question:

How can I serve God today?

_____

_____

_____

_____

Good morning Holy Spirit, will you speak to me today.

Devotional: 3 Reasons You're Winning

1 John 4:4 (KJV)

"Ye are of God, little children, and have overcome them: because greater is he that is in you, than he that is in the world."

#1 You Are of God

You belong to God, and that alone is a reason to celebrate. Being "of God" means you are part of His family, chosen and loved by Him. Your identity is secure in Christ, and nothing in this world can separate you from His love. You are on the winning side because you are His.

#2 God Called You an Overcomer

God declares you victorious before the battle even begins. You've already overcome the challenges of this world because of what Jesus accomplished on the cross. When trials come, remember that you're not fighting for victory—you're fighting from victory. Walk confidently, knowing that overcoming is part of your identity in Christ.

#3 God Is Great in You

The greatness of God's Spirit within you surpasses anything the world can throw at you. His power, wisdom, and strength dwell in you, equipping you to face every challenge. Greater is the One in you than anything opposing you. This truth ensures that no matter the obstacle, God's greatness guarantees your victory.

Prayer

Lord, thank You for making me Yours and calling me an overcomer. Remind me daily that Your greatness in me is far greater than anything in the world. Help me to walk in confidence and victory, knowing that I am secure in You. In Jesus' name, Amen.

Reflection Question

How can you live out your identity as an overcomer today, trusting in God's greatness within you?

Action Question:

How can I serve God today?

Good morning Holy Spirit, will you speak to me today.

Devotional: The Promises of God

2 Corinthians 1:20 (KJV)

"For all the promises of God in him are yea, and in him Amen, unto the glory of God by us."

#1 There Are Promises Over Your Life

God has spoken promises over your life, promises rooted in His Word and His love for you. These promises include provision, protection, peace, and purpose. They remind you of His faithfulness and His plan for your life. Rest in the assurance that His promises are unchanging and meant to bless and guide you.

#2 Your Response to the Promise Is Yes

Every promise of God in Christ is a resounding "yes," but our response matters too. When you say "yes" to His promises, you align your faith with His will. Saying "yes" is an act of trust, believing that what He has spoken will come to pass, even if you don't see it yet.

#3 His Promise Will Bring Him Glory

God's promises are not just for our benefit—they are ultimately for His glory. When His promises are fulfilled in your life, they showcase His faithfulness, power, and love to the world. As you walk in His promises, your life becomes a testimony that glorifies Him and draws others to His goodness.

Prayer

Lord, thank You for the promises You've spoken over my life. Help me to trust Your Word and respond with a confident "yes" in faith. Let Your promises be fulfilled in me in a way that brings glory to Your name and draws others to You. In Jesus' name, Amen.

Reflection Question

What promise of God are you holding onto today, and how can you respond with faith and trust to bring Him glory?

Action Question:

How can I serve God today?

_____

_____

_____

_____

Good morning Holy Spirit, will you speak to me today.

Devotional: Desert Declarations

Psalm 63:1 (KJV)

"O God, thou art my God; early will I seek thee: my soul thirsteth for thee, my flesh longeth for thee in a dry and thirsty land, where no water is."

#1 We Must Own Our God

David begins with a personal declaration: "O God, thou art my God." This is a statement of ownership and intimacy. In every season, especially in the dry and difficult ones, we must reaffirm that God is our God. He isn't distant or detached—He's personal and present, desiring a close relationship with us.

#2 We Must Seek Our God

David's response to the desert wasn't despair; it was pursuit. "Early will I seek thee" reflects a proactive and intentional effort to seek God. Whether you're in a season of abundance or in a wilderness, seeking God first is essential. He promises that when we seek Him with all our hearts, we will find Him (Jeremiah 29:13).

#3 We Must Declare Our Need for Our God

David openly declares his deep need for God: "My soul thirsteth for thee, my flesh longeth for thee." In times of dryness, it's easy to fill our souls with temporary distractions, but only God can truly satisfy. Acknowledging your need for Him is the first step to experiencing His refreshing presence and provision in the desert.

Prayer

Lord, You are my God, and I seek You with all my heart.
In seasons of dryness and thirst, remind me that only You
can satisfy my soul. Help me to declare my need for You
daily and trust that You will meet me wherever I am. In
Jesus' name, Amen.

Reflection Question

What steps can you take today to intentionally seek God
and declare your dependence on Him, even in the dry
seasons of life?

Action Question:

How can I serve God today?

_____

_____

_____

_____

Good morning Holy Spirit, will you speak to me today.

Devotional: Pressing Season

Philippians 3:14 (KJV)

"I press toward the mark for the prize of the high calling of God in Christ Jesus."

#1 Press Toward the Goal

The Christian journey is one of forward motion. Pressing toward the goal means staying focused on what God has called you to do. Distractions, setbacks, and challenges will come, but your goal remains fixed: fulfilling God's purpose for your life. Keep your eyes on Him and continue moving forward, no matter the obstacles.

#2 Press for the Prize

The ultimate reward isn't temporary or earthly—it's eternal. Pressing for the prize means striving for the heavenly reward that God has promised to those who remain faithful. This isn't about earning salvation; it's about living with intentionality, knowing that your efforts for God's kingdom are not in vain.

#3 Press in Christ

Your strength to press forward comes from Christ. Without Him, the challenges of life can overwhelm you. But with Him, you have the power to endure and overcome. Pressing in Christ means relying on His strength, grace, and guidance as you pursue the high calling He has placed on your life.

Prayer

Lord, thank You for calling me to a high purpose in Christ Jesus. Help me to press forward with focus, perseverance, and faith, knowing that You give me the strength to reach the prize. Keep me grounded in You as I pursue Your will for my life. In Jesus' name, Amen.

Reflection Question

What specific goals has God placed in your heart, and how can you press forward in faith and perseverance during this season?

Action Question:

How can I serve God today?

_____

_____

_____

_____

Good morning Holy Spirit, will you speak to me today.

Devotional: Divine Designation

Ephesians 2:10 (KJV)

"For we are his workmanship, created in Christ Jesus unto good works, which God hath before ordained that we should walk in them."

#1 You Were Designed by God

You are not a random creation; you are the workmanship of God. The word "workmanship" implies craftsmanship, intentionality, and care. God created you with precision, placing within you unique abilities, talents, and characteristics. Embrace the truth that you are fearfully and wonderfully made by the Creator of the universe.

#2 You Were Designed with Purpose

God didn't just create you to exist—He created you for a reason. Your life is not accidental or meaningless. You were designed for good works that reflect His character and serve others. Recognize that every step of your life is part of a divine blueprint meant to glorify Him and make a positive impact.

#3 You Were Designed for His Purpose

Your life is ultimately about fulfilling His purpose, not your own. God has ordained specific works for you to walk in, planned long before you were born. When you align your desires and actions with His purpose, you step into a life of meaning and significance that reflects His glory and brings His kingdom closer.

Prayer

Lord, thank You for creating me as Your masterpiece. Help me to embrace the purpose You've placed within me and to live a life that reflects Your glory. Teach me to walk in the good works You've prepared for me, trusting Your plan every step of the way. In Jesus' name, Amen.

Reflection Question

What steps can you take today to align your life with God's purpose and walk in the good works He has designed for you?

Action Question:

How can I serve God today?

_____

_____

_____

_____

Good morning Holy Spirit, will you speak to me today.

Devotional: Do It Big

Colossians 3:23 (KJV)

"And whatsoever ye do, do it heartily, as to the Lord, and not unto men." #1 Do Something

God has given each of us talents, opportunities, and a calling. The first step is to get moving. Whatever you're called to do—big or small—start with faith and determination. Waiting for the "perfect moment" often leads to inaction. Step forward and do something with what God has already placed in your hands.

#2 Do It Big

When you work for the Lord, aim for excellence. Don't hold back or settle for mediocrity. Put your whole heart into your efforts, knowing that you are representing God's kingdom. Whether you're serving in ministry, working a job, or helping a neighbor, go above and beyond to reflect God's greatness.

#3 Do It Unto God

Your ultimate audience isn't people—it's God. When you shift your focus from seeking human approval to honoring Him, your work takes on eternal value. Doing things "unto the Lord" means your effort is an act of worship. Remember, everything you do is an opportunity to glorify God.

Prayer

Lord, help me to step out boldly and use the gifts You've given me. Teach me to do my work with excellence and passion, knowing that I am serving You in all things. May my efforts reflect Your glory and inspire others to see Your greatness. In Jesus' name, Amen.

Reflection Question

What task or calling can you approach today with wholehearted effort, doing it "big" and doing it as an act of worship to God?

Action Question:

How can I serve God today?

_____

_____

_____

_____

Good morning Holy Spirit, will you speak to me today.

Devotional: A Winning Formula

1 Corinthians 16:13 (KJV)

"Watch ye, stand fast in the faith, quit you like men, be strong."

#1 Keep Your Eyes Open

Paul begins with the instruction to "watch." Spiritual vigilance is essential in a world full of distractions and challenges. Stay alert to God's leading, the enemy's schemes, and opportunities to grow and serve. Keeping your eyes open means being aware of your spiritual surroundings and staying grounded in God's truth.

#2 Keep Believing What You Know

To "stand fast in the faith" is to remain steadfast in what you've been taught. Challenges may arise to test your beliefs, but hold firmly to the truth of God's Word. Let your faith be your anchor, trusting in what you know about God's character, promises, and plan, even when the world around you wavers.

#3 Keep Standing Strong

Paul encourages us to "quit you like men" (be courageous) and "be strong." Strength in faith isn't about physical might—it's about spiritual resilience. Draw your strength from God through prayer, Scripture, and fellowship. Stand strong, knowing that God is your foundation and that His strength is made perfect in your weakness.

Prayer

Lord, help me to stay watchful and alert to the challenges and opportunities around me. Strengthen my faith so I can stand firm in what I know to be true. Give me courage and boldness to remain steadfast in You, no matter what comes my way. In Jesus' name, Amen.

Reflection Question

What steps can you take today to stay spiritually alert, stand firm in your faith, and draw strength from God?

Action Question:

How can I serve God today?

_____

_____

_____

_____

Good morning Holy Spirit, will you speak to me today.

Devotional: Fix Your Eyes on Jesus

Hebrews 12:2 (KJV)

"Looking unto Jesus the author and finisher of our faith; who for the joy that was set before him endured the cross, despising the shame, and is set down at the right hand of the throne of God."

#1 Live in Expectation

Jesus endured the cross because of the joy set before Him—He looked ahead to the victory and redemption His sacrifice would bring. As His followers, we are called to live with the same expectation. No matter what challenges you face, know that God is working all things together for good. Fix your eyes on the hope and joy that await you in Him.

#2 Jesus Started It

Jesus is the author of our faith, meaning He initiated this journey with His love and grace. Your faith began because He called you, saved you, and gave you the gift of belief. Remember, He chose you before you could ever choose Him. Trust that what He started in you is intentional and part of His divine plan.

#3 Jesus Will Finish It

Jesus is not just the author but the finisher of our faith. He doesn't leave things incomplete. Whatever He begins, He brings to completion. Trust that He will carry you through every trial and season of life, perfecting your faith and leading you to the eternal joy set before you.

Prayer

Lord, thank You for being the author and finisher of my faith. Teach me to live with expectation, trusting that You are working in and through every situation. Help me to keep my eyes fixed on You, knowing You will carry me through to completion. In Jesus' name, Amen.

Reflection Question

What areas of your life require a renewed focus on Jesus as the one who began and will complete your journey of faith?

Action Question:

How can I serve God today?

_____

_____

_____

_____

Good morning Holy Spirit, will you speak to me today.

Devotional: Whatever You Say

Mark 11:23 (KJV)

"For verily I say unto you, That whosoever shall say unto this mountain, Be thou removed, and be thou cast into the sea; and shall not doubt in his heart, but shall believe that those things which he saith shall come to pass; he shall have whatsoever he saith." #1 Use Your Mouth to Bless You

Your words carry power. When you speak in faith, you align your declarations with God's promises. Instead of allowing your words to reflect fear, doubt, or negativity, use your mouth to declare blessings over your life. Speak life, hope, and victory into your situation, knowing that your words have the ability to shape your reality.

#2 Mountains Will Respond to the Faith in Your Mouth

Jesus didn't tell us to climb the mountain—He told us to speak to it. The challenges in your life aren't meant to intimidate you; they're meant to respond to your faith-filled words. Mountains move when your words are backed by unwavering belief in God's power. Trust that when you speak in alignment with His will, even the biggest obstacles must obey.

#3 There's Victory in Your Mouth

Victory begins with what you believe and declare. When your faith matches your words, you activate God's authority in your life. Speak God's Word over your battles, knowing that He has already secured the victory. With faith in your heart and confidence in your voice, declare that the mountain must move and that God's promises will prevail.

Prayer

Lord, thank You for the power You've given me to speak in faith. Teach me to use my words to bless my life and align with Your promises. Help me to believe without doubting, knowing that mountains will move when I trust in Your power. In Jesus' name, Amen.

Reflection Question

What "mountain" in your life do you need to speak to today, and how can you align your words with God's promises to declare victory?

Action Question:

How can I serve God today?

Good morning Holy Spirit, will you speak to me today.

Devotional: He Cares for You

Psalm 63:1

"Casting all your care upon him; for he careth for you."

#1 Throw It on Him

God invites us to cast—literally throw—our worries, fears, and burdens unto Him. This isn't a gentle handing over but a deliberate act of letting go. When life feels overwhelming, remember that you weren't meant to carry it all. Release it to Him, trusting that He will take care of every concern.

#2 He Can Handle It

Unlike us, God's strength is limitless. No problem is too big, no detail too small for Him to handle. Whatever you're carrying—financial stress, relationship struggles, or uncertainty about the future—He is fully capable of managing it. Trust in His ability to handle what you can't.

#3 Your Cares Are His Cares

God doesn't just take on your burdens because He has to—He does it because He cares deeply for you. Every worry in your heart matters to Him because you matter to Him. Rest in the assurance that your concerns are not just yours anymore; they belong to the One who loves you with an everlasting love.

Prayer

Lord, thank You for caring about every detail of my life. Teach me to cast my burdens onto You, knowing that You are strong enough to handle them and loving enough to carry them. Help me trust in Your care and rest in Your peace. In Jesus' name, Amen.

Reflection Question

What cares or burdens are you holding onto that you need to throw onto God today? How can you trust Him to handle them completely?

Action Question:

How can I serve God today?

_____

_____

_____

_____

Good morning Holy Spirit, will you speak to me today.

Devotional: You're Safe

Psalm 46:4–5 (KJV)

"There is a river, the streams whereof shall make glad the city of God, the holy place of the tabernacles of the most High. God is in the midst of her; she shall not be moved: God shall help her, and that right early."

#1 God Is There

The presence of God is your greatest assurance. Just as the river brings life and joy to the city of God, His presence brings peace and gladness to your heart. No matter where you are or what you face, He is with you. His presence makes you unshakable because the Most High dwells within you.

#2 Your Enemy Won't Win

The Scripture reminds us that God's people "shall not be moved." No attack from the enemy can uproot you when God is your foundation. Your adversaries may try, but their efforts are futile against the One who is in your midst. God's power guarantees that your enemies will not prevail.

#3 His Help Is Eminent

God's help doesn't come late; it comes right on time. His Word promises that He will help you "right early," bringing deliverance and support when you need it most. Trust in His timing, knowing that He sees every detail and is working on your behalf, even now.

Prayer

Lord, thank You for being my constant presence and my ever-present help. Remind me that with You in my midst, I cannot be shaken. Help me to trust that my enemies cannot win and that Your help will arrive exactly when I need it. In Jesus' name, Amen.

Reflection Question

Where in your life do you need to trust God's presence, power, and timely help to remind you that you are truly safe?

Action Question:

How can I serve God today?

_____

_____

_____

_____

Good morning Holy Spirit, will you speak to me today.

Devotional: Winning Thinking

James 4:7 (KJV)

"Submit yourselves therefore to God. Resist the devil, and he will flee from you."

#1 The Plan of God Works

Submission to God is not weakness; it's power. His plan is clear: surrender to His authority, align with His will, and victory will follow. When you trust His way and yield to His guidance, the enemy has no foothold in your life. God's plan always works when we walk in obedience and faith.

#2 No Statement May Be the Loudest Statement

Resisting the devil doesn't always require a loud declaration or physical action. Sometimes, the most powerful response is simply saying "no." Choosing not to engage, react, or give attention to the enemy's schemes is a bold act of defiance. Silence can be the loudest statement when it reflects trust in God's ability to handle the battle.

#3 Take Away the Fuel, the Fire Goes Out

The devil thrives on our fears, doubts, and reactions. When you submit to God and resist the devil, you take away the fuel he needs to stir up chaos. Without attention or cooperation, his influence weakens, and he is forced to flee. Trusting God and standing firm removes the enemy's power to disrupt your life.

Prayer

Lord, help me to fully submit to You and trust Your plan for my life. Teach me to resist the enemy with confidence, knowing that Your power within me is greater than any attack. Let my actions, words, and trust in You extinguish the enemy's schemes. In Jesus' name, Amen.

Reflection Question

What steps can you take today to submit more fully to God and resist the enemy in a way that takes away his influence over your life?

Action Question:

How can I serve God today?

_____

_____

_____

_____

Good morning Holy Spirit, will you speak to me today.

Devotional: Work That Rewards

Proverbs 14:23 (KJV)

"In all labour there is profit: but the talk of the lips tendeth only to penury."

#1 Give It Your All

Hard work brings reward, whether in spiritual growth, personal development, or tangible results. God honors diligence and effort, reminding us that labor produces value. When you commit wholeheartedly to what God has placed before you, you reflect His character and open the door to His blessings.

#2 Give It Your Heart

True labor isn't just about physical effort; it's about working with purpose and passion. When you invest your heart into your work—whether serving others, pursuing a goal, or building God's kingdom—it transforms the task into an act of worship. Your attitude matters as much as your actions.

#3 It Will Give Back to You

The rewards of labor extend beyond material profit. Hard work builds character, strengthens faith, and allows you to experience the satisfaction of doing what God has called you to do. As you give your all and work with the right heart, trust that God will return blessings to you in ways you may not even expect.

Prayer

Lord, thank You for the reminder that all labor has value. Help me to give my all in every task, working with purpose and heart. May my efforts glorify You and bring forth the blessings You have promised. In Jesus' name, Amen.

Reflection Question

How can you approach your work today with greater effort and heart, trusting that God will use it to produce lasting rewards?

Action Question:

How can I serve God today?

_____

_____

_____

_____

Good morning Holy Spirit, will you speak to me today.

Devotional: Plan to Win

Proverbs 16:1 (KJV)

"The preparations of the heart in man, and the answer of the tongue, is from the LORD."

#1 Making Plans Is Important

God has given us the ability to dream, strategize, and prepare. Planning is part of being a good steward of the time and resources He has entrusted to us. While making plans is essential, we must remember that they are just the starting point. Our plans should always leave room for God's guidance.

#2 Praying About Making Plans Is More Important

Planning without prayer is like walking without direction. Before committing to a path, bring your plans to God in prayer. Seek His wisdom and clarity to ensure your decisions align with His will. When you invite Him into the process, He provides insight and peace, even when adjustments are needed.

#3 Let God Have the Last Say-So

Ultimately, the outcome of your plans is in God's hands. Trust that His ways are higher than yours and that His guidance will always lead to the best results. Submitting your plans to Him allows Him to refine and perfect them, ensuring they align with His purpose for your life.

Prayer

Lord, thank You for giving me the ability to plan and prepare. Teach me to seek You first in all my decisions, trusting Your wisdom and guidance. Help me to surrender my plans to You, knowing that Your ways are perfect and Your timing is best. In Jesus' name, Amen.

Reflection Question

How can you invite God into your planning process today, ensuring He has the final say in your decisions?

Action Question:

How can I serve God today?

_____

_____

_____

_____

Good morning Holy Spirit, will you speak to me today.

Devotional: Strength for Possession

Deuteronomy 11:8 (KJV)

"Therefore shall ye keep all the commandments which I command you this day, that ye may be strong, and go in and possess the land, whither ye go to possess it."

#1 God's Word Makes Us Strong

Obedience to God's Word equips us with spiritual strength. Following His commandments builds resilience, fortifies our faith, and prepares us for the challenges ahead. When we align our lives with His truth, we receive the power to stand firm, overcome obstacles, and remain steadfast in His promises.

#2 God's Word Gives Direction

God's commandments are not just rules; they are a roadmap for navigating life. His Word provides clarity and purpose, guiding us toward His perfect will. As you follow His direction, you'll discover the confidence to step forward, knowing that each step is part of His divine plan.

#3 God's Word Is About Possessing the Land

God's promises are meant to be claimed. Obedience opens the door to receiving all that He has prepared for you. The "land" He calls you to possess represents His blessings, purpose, and inheritance for your life. Trusting and applying His Word ensures that you walk boldly into the destiny He has designed for you.

Prayer

Lord, thank You for the strength, direction, and promises found in Your Word. Help me to obey Your commands faithfully, trusting that they prepare me to possess the blessings You have set before me. Strengthen my heart to follow You boldly into the land You've promised. In Jesus' name, Amen.

Reflection Question

What specific step of obedience can you take today to align with God's Word and move closer to possessing His promises for your life?

Action Question:

How can I serve God today?

_____

_____

_____

_____

Good morning Holy Spirit, will you speak to me today.

Devotional: The Blessing of the Lord

Proverbs 10:22 (KJV)

"The blessing of the LORD, it maketh rich, and he addeth no sorrow with it."

1. God Wants to Bless You

God's heart is generous toward His children. He delights in giving good gifts and meeting every need. It's more than just material gain; His blessing covers every aspect of life—spiritual, emotional, and physical. Trust that His intention is to bless you, not harm you, as you walk in faith and obedience.

2. God's Blessing Comes with Increase

When God blesses, it brings growth and abundance. This might be seen in finances, opportunities, relationships, or spiritual maturity. His blessing isn't just about having more but about experiencing a richer, fuller life in Him. Look for ways He is increasing your influence, capacity, or provision as a testimony of His goodness.

3. God's Blessing Comes with Joy

Many strive after material gain, only to find sorrow and emptiness. But the blessing of the Lord adds no sorrow. His gifts come with lasting peace and genuine joy. When God is the source, the outcome is satisfying and free from the regrets or burdens that often accompany worldly success.

Prayer

Lord, thank You for Your desire to bless me abundantly. Open my eyes to see Your blessing in every part of my life, and guard my heart from seeking gain apart from You. May Your gifts bring me joy and draw me closer to Your loving presence. In Jesus' name, Amen.

Reflection Question

Where can you recognize God's blessing in your life today, and how can you embrace it with gratitude and joy?

Action Question:

How can I serve God today?

_____

_____

_____

_____

Good morning Holy Spirit, will you speak to me today.

Devotional: Unstoppable Destiny

Romans 8:31 (KJV)

"What shall we then say to these things? If God be for us, who can be against us?"

1. Your Destiny Has Been Written

God's plan for your life isn't random; it's divinely orchestrated. He has a purpose for you, and that purpose is firmly established by His sovereign will. Knowing your destiny is in His hands frees you from the pressure of trying to control every outcome. Instead, you can trust that He has already penned your story with redemption, hope, and victory.

2. God Is for You

The truth that "God be for us" can revolutionize your mindset. You're not trying to earn His favor or prove your worth—He's already on your side. His love, protection, and guidance are constant companions, even in difficult seasons. When setbacks arise, remembering that God is your advocate gives you confidence to move forward.

3. No One Will Stop You

Because God is for you, no opposition can ultimately succeed against you. Challenges may come, and people may doubt you, but they cannot override God's plan. You don't need to fear or compromise; the same power that raised Christ from the dead is at work in you. Walk boldly, knowing that nothing and no one can thwart God's purpose for your life.

Prayer

Lord, thank You for writing my destiny and standing by me in every circumstance. Teach me to walk confidently in Your plan, knowing that no one can stand against me when You are on my side. Strengthen my faith and help me trust Your heart and guidance daily. In Jesus' name, Amen.

Reflection Question

Which area of your life needs a fresh reminder that God is for you, and how can you walk more boldly in that truth today?

Action Question:

How can I serve God today?

_____

_____

_____

_____

Good morning Holy Spirit, will you speak to me today.

Devotional: Confidence in Asking

1 John 5:14 (KJV)

"And this is the confidence that we have in him, that, if we ask anything according to his will, he heareth us."

1. Ask in Confidence

God invites us to come before Him boldly. You don't need to shrink back or worry about whether He's paying attention—He always is. Confidence comes from knowing that He is both willing and able to hear your prayers. Embrace your identity as His child, and let that assurance guide the way you approach Him.

2. Ask in Faith

Confidence alone isn't enough; it must be paired with faith. When you ask, believe that God has the power to fulfill your request. Whether the answer comes quickly or over time, your faith in His faithfulness keeps you anchored. Trust that His character is unchanging and that He is working everything out for good.

3. Ask According to His Will

The key to answered prayer is alignment with God's will. As you spend time in His Word and remain sensitive to the Holy Spirit, you learn to pray in a way that reflects His heart. When your desires match His purpose, you can rest assured that He hears you and will bring His perfect plan to pass.

Prayer

Lord, thank You for the privilege of asking in confidence, rooted in faith and aligned with Your will. Teach me to seek Your heart above all else, and strengthen my faith to trust Your perfect timing and answers. In Jesus' name, Amen.

Reflection Question

How can you deepen your understanding of God's will so that your prayers align more closely with His heart and purpose?

Action Question:

How can I serve God today?

_____

_____

_____

_____

Good morning Holy Spirit, will you speak to me today.

Devotional: When the Impossible Becomes Possible

Luke 18:27 (KJV)

"And he said, The things which are impossible with men are possible with God."

1. Trust God for What You Think Is Impossible

God specializes in making the impossible possible. When you face obstacles that feel overwhelming, remember that He isn't limited by our resources, logic, or timelines. If you believe your situation is beyond hope, lift your eyes to the One whose power knows no bounds.

2. Life Is Laden with Impossibilities

Every stage of life presents us with challenges that seem insurmountable—whether they're financial burdens, health crises, or strained relationships. These impossibilities can weigh us down. Yet, they're also opportunities for God to display His might and for our faith to grow.

3. Impossibilities Are Not Stop Signs

An impossible situation doesn't mean you should quit. Rather, it's an invitation to rely on God's strength instead of your own. When you encounter a "dead end," consider it a chance to see God intervene in ways beyond human capacity. Remember: your greatest obstacle can become a platform for God's greatest miracle.

Prayer

Lord, thank You for reminding me that nothing is
impossible for You. Help me to trust You completely
when life feels overwhelming. Strengthen my faith as I
turn to You for solutions where I see only dead ends. In
Jesus' name, Amen.

Reflection Question

What impossible situation in your life can you commit to
God today, trusting Him to turn it into an opportunity for
His power to work?

Action Question:

How can I serve God today?

_____

_____

_____

_____

Good morning Holy Spirit, will you speak to me today.

Devotional: For Surely There is an End

Proverbs 23:18

Scripture: "For surely there is an end; and thine expectation shall not be cut off."

#1 It Came to Pass

Life is filled with seasons, and no season lasts forever. The challenges, trials, and waiting periods you face are not permanent—they will come to pass. This truth reminds us to trust in God's timing, knowing that He works all things together for our good. The phrase "it came to pass" appears frequently in the Bible, signaling that every storm has an expiration date. Hold on! Your current situation is not your final destination. God is preparing you for the next chapter of your story.

#2 You Must See It in Your Favor

Faith is about seeing beyond your circumstances and believing in God's promises. Even when things seem uncertain, you must view them through the lens of God's favor. What looks like a setback is often a setup for something greater. The expectation mentioned in Proverbs 23:18 requires faith to see the outcome aligned with God's goodness. Start declaring: "This is working in my favor. God is turning it around for me." Your perspective will fuel your perseverance and keep your hope alive.

#3 God's Gonna Do It

The promise of God's Word is that your expectation will not be cut off. What you're trusting Him for—healing, provision, breakthrough, or restoration—is on its way. God is a promise-keeper, and He finishes what He starts. While the timing may not always match our plans, God's timing is always perfect. Rest in the assurance that God is going to do it. He will complete the good work He began in your life. Stand firm and keep expecting, because God never fails.

Prayer

Father, thank You for the assurance in Your Word that my expectation will not be cut off. Help me to endure the seasons of waiting, trusting that they will come to pass. Open my eyes to see every situation in my favor and give me the faith to believe that You are working all things together for my good. I stand on the promise that You are a faithful God, and I declare that You will do what You've promised in my life. In Jesus' name, Amen.

Reflection

• What challenges are you currently facing that you need to remind yourself "it came to pass"?

• How can you shift your perspective to see God's favor in your situation?

• What promises from God are you holding onto, trusting that He will do it?

Action Question:

How can I serve God today?

Good morning Holy Spirit, will you speak to me today.

Devotional: Walking in the Spirit

Galatians 5:16 (KJV)

"This I say then, Walk in the Spirit, and ye shall not fulfil the lust of the flesh."

1. Your Walk Must Be Important to You

Your daily journey with Christ isn't something to take lightly—it's the heartbeat of your faith. When you value your walk, you intentionally guard it by making choices that honor God. Pay attention to how you spend your time, the habits you form, and the environments you allow into your life. A walk worth protecting is a walk that consistently grows in grace.

2. God's Spirit Must Be Your Regulating Force

Walking in the Spirit means surrendering to the Holy Spirit's guidance. He's your counselor, comforter, and the one who empowers you to choose godly actions. Instead of relying on your own wisdom or strength, let His Word and His voice direct your steps. As He leads, you'll find greater freedom and deeper fulfillment in Christ.

3. The Flesh Must Take a Backseat to the Spirit

The flesh will always clamor for attention, but it shouldn't dictate your decisions. Its desires often conflict with what God desires for you. Letting the Spirit lead means saying "no" to the flesh and "yes" to God's transforming power. The result is a life marked by victory, peace, and fruitfulness for the kingdom.

Prayer

Lord, thank You for giving me the gift of Your Spirit to guide and empower me. Help me to value my spiritual walk and to submit to Your leading each day. Teach me to silence the voice of my flesh and yield to the Holy Spirit's direction, so that I may live a life pleasing to You. In Jesus' name, Amen.

Reflection Question

In which areas of your life do you need to let the Holy Spirit take the lead, allowing the flesh to take a backseat?

Action Question:

How can I serve God today?

_____

_____

_____

_____

Good morning Holy Spirit, will you speak to me today.

Devotional: Planted for Prosperity

Psalm 1:3 (KJV)

"And he shall be like a tree planted by the rivers of water, that bringeth forth his fruit in his season; his leaf also shall not wither; and whatsoever he doeth shall prosper."

1. Where You Dwell Is Ultra Important

Just like a tree thrives when planted by a steady water source, we flourish when rooted in God's presence. The environment you choose—your spiritual community, the influences you allow, the priorities you set—significantly impacts your growth. When you stay near the "rivers" of God's Word and His Spirit, you position yourself to draw life, strength, and nourishment directly from Him.

2. Where You Dig Is Equally Important

A tree needs deep roots for stability and growth. Likewise, you need to dig deep into Scripture, prayer, and fellowship with believers to develop a strong foundation. Shallow roots won't sustain you in life's storms. By investing in spiritual disciplines, you anchor yourself in God's truth, ensuring you remain steadfast when challenges arise.

3. Where You Dwell and Dig Determines Your Outcome

Your fruitfulness and resilience—symbolized by a leaf that does not wither—stem from being both planted and rooted in the right place. When you consistently seek God's presence and dig into His Word, everything you do prospers under His guidance. This doesn't mean a life without trials, but it does mean enduring strength and flourishing through every season.

Prayer

Lord, thank You for being my source of life, strength, and stability. Help me to choose wisely where I dwell, to dig deeply into Your Word, and to trust You for the fruitful outcome You've promised. Let my life bring honor to You in every season. In Jesus' name, Amen.

Reflection Question

Where can you become more intentional about planting yourself in God's presence and digging deeper into His Word so that you experience lasting growth and fruitfulness?

Action Question:

How can I serve God today?

_____

_____

_____

_____

Good morning Holy Spirit, will you speak to me today.

Devotional: The Source

Habakkuk 3:19 (KJV)

"The LORD God is my strength, and he will make my feet like hinds' feet, and he will make me to walk upon mine high places."

1. Recognize the Source

Our ultimate strength comes from God Himself. When you acknowledge Him as the source of your power and hope, you're no longer relying on your own limited abilities. Instead, you tap into His boundless might and provision. Recognizing God as your source changes your perspective on every challenge you face.

2. The Source Will Stabilize You

Just as hinds' feet enable deer to navigate treacherous terrain with ease, God equips you to find stability in life's toughest circumstances. Even when situations feel shaky or uncertain, He provides firm footing. Trust Him to steady your steps and keep you from stumbling.

3. The Source Will Reestablish You

God doesn't just keep you from falling—He elevates you. He promises to make you walk upon the "high places," a picture of renewed position and purpose. Where you felt weak or defeated, He brings restoration and lifts you to places of victory, allowing you to see your situation from His vantage point.

Prayer

Lord, thank You for being my strength and stability. Help me to recognize You as my ultimate source of power and hope. Steady my steps and reestablish me on higher ground, so I may experience the victory You have prepared for me. In Jesus' name, Amen.

Reflection Question

In what area of your life do you need to recognize God as your source, trust Him for stability, and allow Him to lift you to higher ground?

Action Question:

How can I serve God today?

_____

_____

_____

_____

Good morning Holy Spirit, will you speak to me today.

Devotional: The Unfailing Word

Isaiah 40:8 (KJV)

"The grass withereth, the flower fadeth: but the word of our God shall stand for ever."

1. Every Person May Not Come Through

It's natural to lean on those around us—family, friends, mentors—but people, like grass and flowers, are limited. Even with the best intentions, they can't always meet every need or be there in every moment. Recognize that while relationships are valuable, God's constancy goes beyond human capacity.

2. Every Plan May Not Work

We strive, plan, and set goals, but our own strategies can fail. Circumstances change, and unforeseen obstacles arise. What seemed rock-solid can quickly wither away. When our earthly plans falter, we're reminded that our ultimate hope should rest in something unshakable.

3. The Word of God Will Bring You Through

In a world of change and uncertainty, God's Word remains steadfast. Every promise found in Scripture carries eternal weight. When everything else fades, His Word stands firm—guiding, comforting, and sustaining you. Let it be your anchor, bringing you through every season, trial, and transition.

Prayer

Lord, thank You for the eternal power and reliability of Your Word. When people fail and my own plans crumble, help me to remember that Your promises never change. Teach me to stand on Your Word, trusting it to guide and carry me through every circumstance. In Jesus' name, Amen.

Reflection Question

Which specific promise from God's Word can you hold onto today, trusting it will remain firm even if other plans and people fall short?

Action Question:

How can I serve God today?

_____

_____

_____

_____

Good morning Holy Spirit, will you speak to me today.

Devotional: Shielded and Lifted

Psalm 3:3 (KJV)

"But thou, O LORD, art a shield for me; my glory, and the lifter up of mine head."

1. There Is No Enemy Too Great for God

David faced many threats, yet he confidently declared God as his shield. Regardless of how formidable your opposition may seem, remember that God's power surpasses every foe. Lean on Him when you feel overwhelmed, knowing that no enemy stands a chance against His might.

2. Allow God to Shield You from People's Opinions

Sometimes the loudest "enemy" isn't physical danger but the criticisms, doubts, or judgments of others. Instead of letting negative voices define you, let the Lord be your shield. Trust Him to guard your heart, silence the noise, and remind you of your worth in His eyes.

3. God Will Lift Your Head in the Midst of Enemies

God doesn't just protect—He also restores dignity and hope. Even in the presence of adversity, He lifts your head high, reminding you of your identity as His beloved child. He not only shields you from harm but also restores your confidence, even when circumstances seem dire.

Prayer

Lord, thank You for being my shield and the One who lifts my head. Help me to trust in Your power over every enemy, and guard me from the negative opinions of others. Remind me daily that my worth and hope are found in You alone. In Jesus' name, Amen.

Reflection Question

How can you intentionally rely on God as your shield and the lifter of your head when facing criticism or adversity?

Action Question:

How can I serve God today?

_____

_____

_____

_____

Good morning Holy Spirit, will you speak to me today.

Devotional: Hope for an Expected End

Proverbs 23:18 (KJV)

"For surely there is an end; and thine expectation shall not be cut off."

1. It Will End

No matter what season you're going through—whether it's hardship, uncertainty, or waiting—Scripture promises that it won't last forever. God is aware of every detail, and He has set boundaries on how long your trial will endure. This reminder offers hope in the midst of what can feel endless. Trust in His timing, knowing that every challenge has a conclusion.

2. It Ends Based on the Plan

God's plan for your life is intentional. He orchestrates each chapter according to His purposes. Even when the path seems unclear, you can trust that He is working behind the scenes, weaving every circumstance into a tapestry that ultimately benefits you and glorifies Him. Since He holds the blueprint, you can rest in the knowledge that He will bring your situation to the right ending.

3. God Knows What You Expect

Your deepest hopes and expectations aren't hidden from God. He values the desires of your heart and knows exactly what you're believing for. As you align your expectations with His promises, you'll find peace in the assurance that He not only sees your needs but delights in meeting them in ways that exceed what you could ask or imagine.

Prayer

Lord, thank You for the promise that every season has its end and that my expectations are safe in Your hands. Help me trust Your plan, even when I don't see how things will resolve. Strengthen my faith so I can wait confidently, knowing You will bring about a good and timely conclusion to every challenge. In Jesus' name, Amen.

Reflection Question

Where do you need to trust God today, believing that He has a purposeful end to your situation and is mindful of your deepest expectations?

Action Question:

How can I serve God today?

_____

_____

_____

_____

Good morning Holy Spirit, will you speak to me today.

Devotional: Powered by God

Philippians 2:13

"For it is God which worketh in you both to will and to do of his good pleasure."

1. God Will Give You the Energy

You don't have to rely solely on your own strength or motivation. God is at work within you, empowering you to do more than you could ever accomplish on your own. His Spirit energizes you not only to desire what's right but also to carry it out. When you feel weak or unmotivated, remember that He provides the power to move forward.

2. You Must Develop the Determination

While God supplies the energy, you play a part by setting your heart on obedience. Determination is your active response to the grace He gives. It's your "yes" to God's prompting. Cultivate habits of prayer, reading Scripture, and surrounding yourself with godly influences. These practices help you stay determined to follow His leading, even when circumstances get tough.

3. Get the Work Done

God doesn't just give you the desire—He wants you to translate that desire into action. Once you sense His prompting and feel His strength fueling you, step out in faith. Whether it's serving in a ministry, showing kindness to a neighbor, or pursuing a new God-honoring goal, follow through with what He's placed on your heart.

You'll discover both joy and fulfillment as you do the work He's prepared for you.

Prayer

Lord, thank You for working within me and supplying both the desire and the strength to follow Your will. Help me to stay determined when challenges arise and to faithfully carry out the tasks You've placed before me. May my actions reflect Your goodness and bring glory to Your name. In Jesus' name, Amen.

Reflection Question

In what specific area of your life do you need to lean on God's energy and determination to get the work done? How can you begin taking action today?

Action Question:

How can I serve God today?

_____

_____

_____

_____

Good morning Holy Spirit, will you speak to me today.

Devotional: Fearless in Him

Psalm 27:1 (KJV)

"The LORD is my light and my salvation; whom shall I fear? the LORD is the strength of my life; of whom shall I be afraid?"

1. God Will Illuminate the Path

When darkness clouds your way—whether through confusion, worry, or uncertainty—God shines His light into every corner. He provides wisdom and guidance so you don't have to stumble blindly. As you seek Him, trust that He will reveal the next steps, giving you clarity and direction in life's hardest moments.

2. God Will Shield You Through the Trouble

Trouble is inevitable, but with the Lord by your side, you have nothing to fear. His protective hand remains upon you, acting as a shield from the storms that rage around you. Though challenges may arise, His presence secures you, assuring you that you're never facing trials alone.

3. God Will Give You the Strength to Finish

Life's journey can be exhausting, yet the Lord promises renewed strength. He doesn't merely light your way or shield you from harm; He empowers you to keep going. Lean on Him when you feel weary, knowing that His strength is made perfect in your weakness—and that He will see you through to victory.

Prayer

Lord, thank You for being my light, my salvation, and my strength. When I feel lost, shine Your wisdom on my path. When trouble strikes, be my shield. And when I'm weary, renew my strength. I trust You to guide me safely and help me finish strong. In Jesus' name, Amen.

Reflection Question

Where do you need God's light, His protection, or His empowering strength today? How can you depend on Him in that specific area?

Action Question:

How can I serve God today?

_____

_____

_____

_____

Good morning Holy Spirit, will you speak to me today.

Devotional: Winning the Unseen Battle

2 Corinthians 10:4 (KJV)

"For the weapons of our warfare are not carnal, but mighty through God to the pulling down of strong holds."

1. You Are in an Extraordinary Fight

As believers, we are engaged in a spiritual conflict that goes beyond ordinary human struggles. Our real battle isn't merely against people or circumstances, but against spiritual strongholds that seek to undermine our faith. Recognizing the extraordinary nature of this fight prepares us to stand firm and not be caught off guard.

2. You Have an Exclusive Arsenal

God has equipped us with spiritual weapons—prayer, the Word of God, faith, worship, and the name of Jesus, among others. These are not man-made tools but divinely empowered resources that effectively dismantle the enemy's strategies. No worldly invention can compare to the exclusive arsenal God provides to those who trust in Him.

3. You Have Divine Excessive Power

Our strength doesn't come from ourselves; it comes "through God." This means we're operating in a power far exceeding human limits. When you stand in God's might, you aren't fighting alone. His unstoppable power goes before you, enabling you to pull down every spiritual stronghold and walk in victory.

Prayer

Lord, thank You for equipping me with spiritual weapons that are mighty through You. Remind me daily that my battle is not against flesh and blood, and help me rely on Your overwhelming power. Let every stronghold crumble as I stand in faith, trusting You for the victory. In Jesus' name, Amen.

Reflection Question

Where in your life do you need to apply God's spiritual weapons today, trusting His divine power to break down strongholds and secure the victory?

Action Question:

How can I serve God today?

_____

_____

_____

_____

Good morning Holy Spirit, will you speak to me today.

Devotional: Satisfied in Every Season

Isaiah 58:11 (KJV)

"And the LORD shall guide thee continually, and satisfy thy soul in drought, and make fat thy bones: and thou shalt be like a watered garden, and like a spring of water, whose waters fail not."

1. God Is Always Leading You

Even when you can't see the next step, God is actively guiding you. His presence doesn't wax or wane based on your circumstances. Whether on a mountaintop of success or in a valley of uncertainty, trust that He is the One charting your course. Draw close in prayer and obedience, knowing that He never leaves you to wander alone.

2. Dry Places Won't Affect You

Drought symbolizes lack and barrenness. Yet, God promises to "satisfy thy soul in drought." When external conditions seem bleak or resources run low, His provision is unwavering. You don't have to fear emptiness because God's streams of grace, peace, and joy are constantly flowing to refresh and renew you.

3. He'll Strengthen You Through It

God won't merely sustain you; He'll "make fat thy bones." That's a vivid picture of nourishment and strength. He empowers you to flourish like a well-watered garden, full of life and growth. In every challenging season, He reinforces your inner foundation so you can endure—and even thrive—no matter what comes your way.

Prayer

Lord, thank You for leading me day by day and for satisfying my soul even in the driest seasons. Strengthen me with Your presence and help me trust that You will provide everything I need. Let my life bloom like a watered garden, reflecting Your grace and power for all to see. In Jesus' name, Amen.

Reflection Question

How can you lean more on God's guidance and provision today, trusting Him to satisfy you even in life's darkest moments?

Action Question:

How can I serve God today?

_____

_____

_____

_____

Good morning Holy Spirit, will you speak to me today.

Devotional: Mind, Peace, and Trust

Isaiah 26:3 (KJV)

"Thou wilt keep him in perfect peace, whose mind is stayed on thee: because he trusteth in thee."

1. Keep Your Mind Right

Our thoughts shape our reality. When we fix our minds on God—His character, promises, and faithfulness—we filter out the noise that leads to anxiety and doubt. A mind "stayed" on the Lord isn't easily swayed by fear or worry. Instead, it is anchored in the truth of His Word.

2. Peace Is the Goal

The outcome of a God-centered mind is perfect peace. This peace goes beyond mere calmness; it's a steady assurance that arises from knowing God is in control. Even in chaos, you can experience tranquility because your focus is on the One who holds your future in His hands.

3. Trust Is the Road

Trusting God is how you move from turmoil to peace. As you rely on His wisdom and power rather than your own understanding, you'll find that uncertainty and fear lose their grip on your heart. Trust is the pathway that leads you to rest in His perfect plan, no matter the circumstances.

Prayer

Lord, help me keep my mind fixed on You so I can experience the perfect peace You promise. Teach me to trust You fully, allowing Your presence to rule over my thoughts and emotions. Thank You for being my source of strength and security. In Jesus' name, Amen.

Reflection Question

In what specific area of your life do you need to shift your focus from fear to trust, so that you can experience God's perfect peace?

Action Question:

How can I serve God today?

_____

_____

_____

_____

Good morning Holy Spirit, will you speak to me today.

Devotional: The God Who Goes Before You

Deuteronomy 31:8 (KJV)

"And the LORD, he it is that doth go before thee; he will be with thee, he will not fail thee, neither forsake thee: fear not, neither be dismayed."

1. God Knows What You're About to Face

Before you step into any new challenge, God is already there. He sees the obstacles and trials ahead, and He's fully prepared to guide you through them. Knowing that God goes before you should give you confidence—He's not caught off guard by anything you will encounter.

2. Your Help Is Sure

Because God goes before you, His help is guaranteed. He has promised never to fail or abandon you. When fear creeps in, remember that His presence is your shield. You don't have to rely on your own strength; He's committed to walking beside you, steadying and supporting you every step of the way.

3. He's the Real Deal

Some promises fade, and some people falter, but God's word never does. He is faithful and unchanging. When He says He'll be there, He means it. We can trust Him because He's proven Himself time and again—He is the same yesterday, today, and forever. There's no need to fear or be dismayed when you know you're backed by the One who never fails.

Prayer

Lord, thank You for going before me and preparing the way. Remind me today that Your presence is my security, and Your promises never change. Help me to trust You wholeheartedly, without fear or dismay, knowing that You're with me every step of my journey. In Jesus' name, Amen.

Reflection Question

What specific area of your life do you need to trust God with today, knowing He's already gone before you and will not fail you?

Action Question:

How can I serve God today?

_____

_____

_____

_____

Good morning Holy Spirit, will you speak to me today.

Devotional: A Reason to Praise

Exodus 15:2 (KJV)

"The LORD is my strength and song, and he is become my salvation: he is my God, and I will prepare him an habitation; my father's God, and I will exalt him."

1. He's My Strength

Life can wear us down, but God's power is limitless. When we feel weak, discouraged, or overwhelmed, He is the One who lifts us up and renews our energy. By relying on His might, we discover we can do more than we ever thought possible. He is the source of the endurance and resilience we need to face every challenge.

2. He's My Song

God isn't just a distant helper; He's also our joy and melody in life. As our "song," He brings purpose and praise into our hearts. Like a soundtrack that uplifts our spirit, His presence transforms even the darkest moments into opportunities to worship. Let your life's anthem be one of gratitude and honor to Him.

3. He's My Victory

True salvation and victory come from the Lord. He rescues us not only in big, dramatic ways but also in the small battles we face daily. Each triumph is a reminder that we are not alone—He goes before us, stands beside us, and ensures that we walk in His overcoming power.

Prayer

Lord, thank You for being my strength, my song, and my victory. Help me to lean on Your power when I'm weak, to sing Your praises in every season, and to trust Your deliverance in every challenge. May my life be a constant reflection of gratitude for all You've done. In Jesus' name, Amen.

Reflection Question

Which aspect of God's character—His strength, His joy, or His saving power—do you need to focus on most right now, and how can you express praise for that today?

Action Question:

How can I serve God today?

_____

_____

_____

_____

Good morning Holy Spirit, will you speak to me today.

Devotional: Abounding in Hope

Romans 15:13 (KJV)

"Now the God of hope fill you with all joy and peace in believing, that ye may abound in hope, through the power of the Holy Ghost."

1. He Will Give You Uncontrollable Joy

God is the source of genuine joy—not a fleeting emotion, but a deep wellspring that overflows even in challenging seasons. When you place your faith in Him, He infuses your heart with a joy that can't be contained. This joy transcends circumstances because it's anchored in who He is, not in what's happening around you.

2. He Will Give You Undeniable Peace

True peace isn't just the absence of conflict; it's the calm assurance that comes from knowing God is in control. When you believe in His promises, your soul finds rest in His sovereignty. His peace dispels worry and anxiety, enabling you to navigate life's storms with steady confidence.

3. He Will Give You Unexplained Abundance of hope

God doesn't merely offer enough hope to get by—He causes you to abound in hope. Through the Holy Spirit's power, He enlarges your capacity to trust, dream, and expect good things from Him. This abundance isn't limited to material blessings; it's an overflow of spiritual vitality that enriches every area of your life.

Prayer

Lord, thank You for being the God of hope who fills me with uncontrollable joy, undeniable peace, and a plentiful supply of hope. Help me to rely on Your Holy Spirit daily, trusting Your power to work in and through me. May my life reflect the abundance You've promised, bringing glory to Your name. In Jesus' name, Amen.

Reflection Question

Which aspect of God's gift—His joy, His peace, or His abundant hope—do you need to embrace more fully today, and how will you intentionally lean into the Holy Spirit's power to receive it?

Action Question:

How can I serve God today?

_____

_____

_____

_____

Good morning Holy Spirit, will you speak to me today.

Devotional: Love in Action

Hebrews 10:24 (KJV)

"And let us consider one another to provoke unto love
and to good works."

1. Love Is Considerate

Genuine love thinks beyond itself. When Scripture says,
"let us consider one another," it invites us to be
thoughtful, observant, and mindful of others' needs. True
love looks for ways to uplift, encourage, and bless those
around us. By putting ourselves in another's shoes, we
learn how to show kindness in ways that truly matter.

2. Love Is Provoking

In this passage, "provoke" doesn't mean to irritate but to
stir up or spur on. Love nudges us—and others—toward
acts of kindness and compassion. When we demonstrate
God's love, we motivate others to do the same. Think of it
like a spark that ignites a chain reaction, inspiring love
and good works in those who witness our actions.

3. Love Is Doing Good

Love doesn't settle for mere words; it's practical and
productive. When we care for someone, we find tangible
ways to meet their needs, whether through prayer,
support, or a helping hand. "Doing good" means turning
our affection into action, reflecting God's own love that
not only felt compassion but took action to redeem us.

Prayer

Lord, thank You for teaching me to love in a way that truly considers others, stirs up compassion, and results in good works. Guide me to see those around me through Your eyes and to respond in practical ways that bring them closer to You. In Jesus' name, Amen.

Reflection Question

In what specific ways can you "provoke" someone to love and do good works today, turning your considerate affection into practical action?

Action Question:

How can I serve God today?

_____

_____

_____

_____

Good morning Holy Spirit, will you speak to me today.

Devotional: Keep the Faith

Matthew 21:22 (KJV)

"And all things, whatsoever ye shall ask in prayer, believing, ye shall receive."

1. Don't Stop Believing

Faith is the foundation of answered prayer. When you believe, you're trusting God to act according to His character and promises. It might not happen in your timing or the way you expect, but God always responds to genuine faith. Keep believing He will fulfill His Word in your life.

2. Don't Stop Dreaming

God honors big prayers and bold dreams. If your vision or goals feel too large for you, that might be exactly where God wants to work. Instead of settling for what seems possible by human standards, invite God to show you His limitless power. Let your dreams reflect His greatness.

3. Don't Stop Praying

Prayer is your lifeline to God's heart. It's not just about asking, but also about listening and aligning your will with His. When you continue in prayer, you create space for God's guidance, comfort, and miraculous intervention. Persist in prayer, and trust that He hears you even when there's a delay in the answers.

Prayer

Lord, thank You for inviting me to come to You with faith-filled prayers and bold dreams. Strengthen my belief when doubt tries to creep in, and help me trust Your perfect timing. Remind me not to give up on prayer, knowing You are always listening and ready to move in my life. In Jesus' name, Amen.

Reflection Question

Where might you need to refresh your belief, expand your dreams, or persevere in prayer today, trusting God for the outcome?

Action Question:

How can I serve God today?

_____

_____

_____

_____

Good morning Holy Spirit, will you speak to me today.

Devotional: Embracing Wisdom

Proverbs 4:6 (KJV)

"Forsake her not, and she shall preserve thee: love her, and she shall keep thee."

1. Wisdom Is Necessary

Wisdom is more than intelligence or knowledge—it's applying God's truth in everyday situations. When you seek His perspective, you navigate life with greater discernment and clarity. Whether in relationships, decisions, or challenges, wisdom illuminates the path you should walk.

2. Wisdom Will Shield You

Life is filled with pitfalls and temptations, but wisdom acts as a protective barrier. By leaning on God's principles, you can avoid unnecessary conflicts, harmful entanglements, and regrets. His wisdom keeps you from being derailed by impulsive or shortsighted choices.

3. Wisdom Will Cover You

To "cover" implies safety and care. Wisdom provides exactly that, offering divine insight that guards your reputation, integrity, and future. When you nurture a love for God's wisdom, you place yourself under the shelter of His guidance, ensuring you're covered in every circumstance.

Prayer

Lord, thank You for the gift of wisdom that protects and guides me. Help me to value it above all earthly knowledge and to apply it faithfully in my everyday life. Teach me to rely on Your Word and Spirit for discernment, trusting that wisdom will shield and cover me. In Jesus' name, Amen.

Reflection Question

Where in your life do you need God's wisdom today, and how can you intentionally seek and apply it for your protection and growth?

Action Question:

How can I serve God today?

_____

_____

_____

_____

Good morning Holy Spirit, will you speak to me today.

Devotional: Under His Shadow

Psalm 91:1 (KJV)

"He that dwelleth in the secret place of the most High shall abide under the shadow of the Almighty."

1. Choose to Dwell with Him

God extends an open invitation to draw close and remain in His presence. Dwelling isn't a casual visit but a deliberate, ongoing choice to spend time with Him. Whether through prayer, worship, or meditation on Scripture, making space for God in your daily life allows you to experience His nearness and guidance.

2. His Choice Is to Cover You

As you settle into His "secret place," God promises His protective covering—His shadow. This divine shelter isn't just for crisis moments; it's your constant refuge. God is more than willing to surround you with His care. By choosing to dwell with Him, you align yourself with His choice to shield you from harm and bring you peace.

Prayer

Lord, thank You for inviting me into Your secret place. Help me to choose to dwell with You daily, knowing that You are eager to cover and protect me. Teach me to rest in Your presence and trust the shelter of Your unfailing love. In Jesus' name, Amen.

Reflection Question

In what practical ways can you choose to dwell more consistently in God's presence, trusting Him to cover and protect you in every season?

Action Question:

How can I serve God today?

_____

_____

_____

_____

Good morning Holy Spirit, will you speak to me today.

Devotional: Abiding in Christ's Peace

John 14:27 (KJV)

"Peace I leave with you, my peace I give unto you: not as the world giveth, give I unto you. Let not your heart be troubled, neither let it be afraid."

1. Jesus Will Be Your Peace

The kind of peace Jesus offers isn't fleeting or dependent on circumstances. It's a deep, abiding tranquility that stems from knowing you are securely held in His hands. When storms rage around you, remember Christ stands with you, offering a calm the world cannot replicate.

2. Jesus Will Be Your Comfort

Jesus' presence brings comfort. In moments of grief, stress, or uncertainty, He becomes the refuge you can run to. His comfort isn't just a pat on the back—it's a steady reassurance that He has overcome the world and walks with you through every valley.

3. Jesus Dispels Your Fear

Fear may knock on the door of your heart, but it doesn't have to stay. As you lean on Jesus, His perfect love casts out all fear. When you trust in His power and sovereignty, fear diminishes because you know the One who holds your future is infinitely greater than any challenge you face.

Prayer

Lord, thank You for the peace You freely give—a peace that surpasses all understanding and is unlike anything the world can offer. Remind me daily that You are my comfort and the One who dispels my fears. Help me to trust in Your presence and power, allowing Your peace to rule in my heart. In Jesus' name, Amen.

Reflection Question

Where in your life do you need to invite Jesus' peace, comfort, and fear-dispelling power today? How can you practically rest in His promise of peace?

Action Question:

How can I serve God today?

_____

_____

_____

_____

Good morning Holy Spirit, will you speak to me today.

Devotional: Seeking the Lord for Deliverance

Psalm 34:4 (KJV)

"I sought the LORD, and he heard me, and delivered me from all my fears." 1. Never Leave Your Life in Others' Hands

We often rely on people—friends, family, or mentors—to guide or rescue us. While these relationships are valuable, they shouldn't take the place of seeking God first. Your trust belongs ultimately to the One who holds your future. Look to Him for wisdom and deliverance instead of making others responsible for your well-being.

2. Pray Until Something Happens

Persistence in prayer is powerful. Keep bringing your fears, anxieties, and questions to the Lord, believing He is actively working even when you can't see immediate results. God loves heartfelt, persistent prayer—don't give up just because you haven't seen a quick turnaround. Press in until you sense His hand moving on your behalf.

3. More "FaceTime," Less Fear Time

Fears grow when we focus on them, but they shrink when we spend time in God's presence. Trade your worry sessions for worship sessions. Let your "face time" with God—through prayer, Bible study, and worship—occupy the space where fear tries to reside. In His presence, fear loses its grip.

Prayer

Lord, thank You for hearing me when I call and for delivering me from my fears. Help me to rely on You first and foremost, to persist in prayer, and to spend more time seeking Your face rather than feeding my fears. Strengthen my faith as I draw closer to You. In Jesus' name, Amen.

Reflection Question

What fear can you hand over to God today, and how will you replace that "fear time" with intentional "face time" in His presence?

Action Question:

How can I serve God today?

_____

_____

_____

_____

Good morning Holy Spirit, will you speak to me today.

Devotional: Bread of Life

John 6:35 (KJV)

"And Jesus said unto them, I am the bread of life: he that cometh to me shall never hunger; and he that believeth on me shall never thirst."

1. Keep Coming

Jesus invites us to come to Him continually, not just once. Just as our bodies need daily nourishment, our souls need consistent fellowship with Christ. Make "coming to Him" a rhythm in your life—through prayer, worship, and time in His Word. In His presence, you find spiritual sustenance that satisfies.

2. Keep Believing

Faith isn't a one-time decision; it's a daily posture of trust. Life's challenges may shake your confidence, but when you keep believing in His promises, you stand on solid ground. Continual belief fuels your relationship with Christ and opens the door for God's power to work in you.

3. You'll Never Starve

Jesus promises that if you come to Him and believe, you will never hunger or thirst spiritually. No matter what emptiness you face, He fills the void with His life-giving presence. When you rely on Christ daily, He satisfies you in ways the world can't. Your soul remains nourished, secure, and complete in Him.

Prayer

Lord, thank You for being the bread of life who meets every spiritual need. Help me to come to You consistently, believe in You unwaveringly, and find true satisfaction in Your presence. May my heart be filled with Your abundant life each day. In Jesus' name, Amen.

Reflection Question

In what practical ways can you "keep coming" to Jesus and "keep believing" so that your soul remains well-fed and satisfied?

Action Question:

How can I serve God today?

_____

_____

_____

_____

Good morning Holy Spirit, will you speak to me today.

Devotional: Because of Him

Psalm 27:1 (KJV)

"The LORD is my light and my salvation; whom shall I fear? the LORD is the strength of my life; of whom shall I be afraid?"

1. Because of Him, I Can See

God's light pierces through the darkness, providing guidance and clarity. Without His illumination, we stumble around in confusion or doubt. When you let the Lord shine in every corner of your life—your thoughts, decisions, and relationships—He reveals the right path and gives you the vision to move forward in faith.

2. Because of Him, I Am Free

Salvation in Christ is the ultimate freedom. We're no longer bound by fear of judgment or guilt from our past. He breaks every chain that once held us captive, allowing us to live boldly and confidently in His grace. Because of Him, you can face each day unshackled by the weights that once held you down.

3. Because of Him, No More Fear

God's presence and strength silence the voices of fear. When the Lord is the foundation of your life, you stand on unshakable ground. You can confront challenges, setbacks, and the unknown with a courage rooted in His power rather than your own. With Him as your light, your salvation, and your stronghold, fear loses its grip.

Prayer

Lord, thank You for being my light, my freedom, and my strength. Help me to see life through Your illuminating grace and to walk free from every chain. Remind me daily that, because of You, I have no reason to fear. In Jesus' name, Amen.

Reflection Question

Which area of your life needs God's light and strength right now, and how can acknowledging His presence help you overcome fear in that specific situation?

Action Question:

How can I serve God today?

_____

_____

_____

_____

Good morning Holy Spirit, will you speak to me today.

Devotional: The Good Life

Hebrews 13:5–6 (KJV)

"Let your conversation be without covetousness; and be content with such things as ye have: for he hath said, I will never leave thee, nor forsake thee. So that we may boldly say, The Lord is my helper, and I will not fear what man shall do unto me."

1. Live in Contentment

God calls us to be free from covetousness—a desire for what others have. Instead, we're encouraged to be satisfied with our present blessings. Contentment is a posture of trust, acknowledging that God knows exactly what we need and provides accordingly. When we embrace this truth, we release the burden of comparison and step into gratitude for what He's already given.

2. Walk in Peace

The promise "I will never leave thee, nor forsake thee" is a perpetual reminder that God's presence is your constant source of peace. His nearness means you never walk alone. In every challenge or uncertainty, His reassuring presence calms your spirit and offers unshakeable peace.

3. Stand in Confidence

Because the Lord is your helper, you don't need to fear any circumstance or opposition. This divine partnership emboldens you to face challenges head-on. When you truly believe that God is for you, you can stand in confidence, free from worry about what others may do or say.

4. Rest in Faith

Knowing God is ever-present and fully dependable allows you to rest in faith rather than fret in anxiety. Release your concerns into His capable hands. Whether you face financial strains, relational tensions, or personal uncertainties, trust that He has you covered. This restful faith positions you to experience His peace and witness His power at work.

Prayer

Lord, teach me the beauty of contentment and the peace that comes from knowing You'll never leave me. Strengthen my confidence to trust in Your help and to stand firm against all fears. Let my heart find rest in the faith that You are always with me. In Jesus' name, Amen.

Reflection Question

Where do you need to embrace more contentment and rest in God's promise that He will never leave nor forsake you?

Action Question:

How can I serve God today?

_____

_____

_____

_____

Good morning Holy Spirit, will you speak to me today.

Devotional: The Nearness of God

Psalm 34:18 (KJV)

"The LORD is nigh unto them that are of a broken heart;
and saveth such as be of a contrite spirit."

1. There He Is

In moments of heartbreak and pain, it can feel like God is
distant—but this verse reminds us He is actually closest
when we're at our lowest. He draws near to our hurts,
never ignoring or minimizing our struggles. If your heart
feels broken, know that His presence is right there,
wrapping you in His comforting love.

2. He's Here to Fix It

God doesn't just sit with us in our brokenness; He
actively works to heal and restore us. His desire is to
mend the pieces of our shattered hearts and bring
wholeness where pain once ruled. He sees every
wound—physical, emotional, or spiritual—and offers His
powerful, life-giving touch.

3. He's Here to Make You Whole

Salvation involves more than just forgiveness of sins; it's
the transformation and renewal of our entire being. As
He repairs your brokenness, He also restores your hope.
In His presence, broken hearts find healing and contrite
spirits are lifted. God's ultimate goal is to make you whole
in every area of your life.

Prayer

Lord, thank You for being close to me when my heart is broken and my spirit is low. Help me trust that You're not just present, but also actively healing and restoring me. I invite Your power to make me whole, renewing my hope in You. In Jesus' name, Amen.

Reflection Question

Where in your life do you need God's healing touch, and how can you invite Him to draw near and make you whole?

Action Question:

How can I serve God today?

_____

_____

_____

_____

Good morning Holy Spirit, will you speak to me today.

Devotional: Embracing Today

Psalm 118:24 (KJV)

"This is the day which the LORD hath made; we will rejoice and be glad in it."

1. Thank God for This Day

Each morning is a gift from God—an opportunity for a new start, fresh mercy, and renewed purpose. Take a moment to express gratitude for waking up, for the breath in your lungs, and for the blessings that often go unnoticed. Recognizing God as the source of every good thing turns an ordinary day into a celebration of His grace.

2. Rejoice in This Day

We're invited not just to acknowledge the day, but to rejoice in it. Joy is a choice that stems from trusting God's goodness rather than focusing on life's challenges. When you decide to find reasons to praise Him—no matter your circumstances—you're declaring that God's faithfulness outweighs any difficulty you face.

3. Make the Best of This Day

God created this day with purpose. Instead of merely going through the motions, approach each hour with intentionality. Love someone in need, speak encouragement, or spend a few extra moments with the Lord in prayer. Ask Him to guide you in making this day count for His glory and your growth.

Prayer

Lord, thank You for this day You have made. Help me to approach it with gratitude, rejoicing in the small and big blessings alike. Show me how to make the most of every moment, and let my actions reflect Your love and goodness. In Jesus' name, Amen.

Reflection Question

How can you shift your mindset today to focus on gratitude, joy, and purposeful action, making this day truly count for God's glory?

Action Question:

How can I serve God today?

_____

_____

_____

_____

Good morning Holy Spirit, will you speak to me today.

Devotional: Ready in Troubled Times

Psalm 20:1 (KJV)

"The LORD hears thee in the day of trouble; the name of the God of Jacob defend thee."

1. Don't Be Surprised by Trouble

Challenges are part of life's journey. While we often hope to avoid hardships, Jesus Himself reminded us that troubles would come. Rather than being caught off guard or discouraged, recognize that adversity is an opportunity for growth and a place where you can experience God's grace in profound ways.

2. God Hears When You Call

Though difficulty may arise, you have a direct line to the Almighty. When you cry out to God, be assured that He listens. He's not distant or disinterested; He cares deeply about every detail of your life. Call on Him with confidence, knowing your prayers do not fall on deaf ears.

3. God Is Ready to Defend You

The psalmist reminds us that "the name of the God of Jacob defends thee." When opposition comes—be it external circumstances or internal struggles—God stands as your shield. His protection may not always look the way you expect, but trust that He is ready and able to guard you from harm, strengthen your heart, and lead you to victory.

Prayer

Lord, thank You for hearing me whenever I call,
especially in times of trouble. Help me to trust in Your
readiness to defend and protect me. Teach me to depend
on Your power, not my own, and to find peace in knowing
You are always near. In Jesus' name, Amen.

Reflection Question

What trouble or challenge do you need to bring before
God today, trusting Him to hear and defend you in your
time of need?

Action Question:

How can I serve God today?

_____

_____

_____

_____

Good morning Holy Spirit, will you speak to me today.

Devotional: Wholistic Prosperity

3 John 1:2 (KJV)

"Beloved, I wish above all things that thou mayest prosper and be in health, even as thy soul prospereth."

1. Prosperity Belongs to You

God's desire is for you to experience well-being in every area of life. Prosperity is not just material abundance; it includes peace of mind, healthy relationships, and spiritual richness. As His beloved child, you have the privilege of walking in the blessings He's prepared for you—body, mind, and spirit.

2. Your Prosperity Is Important to God

Some imagine God as distant or unconcerned with practical matters, but His Word shows otherwise. God cares about your financial stability, your emotional health, and your overall success. When you align your life with His principles and purpose, you invite His blessings into every aspect of your existence.

3. Wholistic Prosperity Is the Goal

Biblical prosperity isn't one-dimensional; it's comprehensive—covering soul, body, and spirit. True prosperity includes a thriving spiritual life, healthy emotions, strong relationships, and the ability to steward resources wisely. Seek God in all these areas, trusting that He wants you to flourish fully.

Prayer

Lord, thank You for desiring my prosperity in every aspect of life. Help me to seek You first, trusting that as my soul prospers, every other area will thrive. Teach me to steward the blessings You provide with wisdom and gratitude, for Your glory. In Jesus' name, Amen.

Reflection Question

Which area of your life—spiritual, emotional, physical, or financial—needs God's touch today so you can experience the holistic prosperity He desires for you?

Action Question:

How can I serve God today?

_____

_____

_____

_____

Good morning Holy Spirit, will you speak to me today.

Devotional: Fully Provided For

Psalm 23:1 (KJV)

"The LORD is my shepherd; I shall not want." 1. The Lord Is

Before anything else, know that God is—He exists, He reigns, and He is intimately involved in your life. His very being is constant and unchanging. When you grasp what He is, you realize you have a foundation that won't shift, no matter what happens around you.

2. My

This Shepherd isn't distant or merely a concept—He is yours. He knows your name, sees your circumstances, and cares about your heart. "My" signifies personal relationship. It's one thing to believe in a shepherd; it's another to claim Him as your own, trusting Him for every detail of your journey.

3. Shepherd

A shepherd leads, protects, and provides. He cares for the flock, ensuring they lack nothing essential. As your Shepherd, God guides you on the right path, shields you from unseen dangers, and supplies everything necessary for your physical, emotional, and spiritual well-being.

4. I Have All I Need

When the Lord is truly your Shepherd, you can say with confidence, "I shall not want." It doesn't mean life is free of challenges, but it does mean you're assured of His provision and presence. With Him, there's no true lack—He meets every need according to His wisdom and love.

Prayer

Lord, thank You for being my Shepherd. Remind me daily that in You I have everything I need. Help me to trust Your guidance, rely on Your protection, and rest in Your abundant care. Teach me to find contentment in Your presence, knowing that You are enough. In Jesus' name, Amen.

Reflection Question

Which aspect of God's shepherd-like care do you need to embrace more today—His guidance, His protection, or His provision—and how will you practically trust Him in that area?

Action Question:

How can I serve God today?

_____

_____

_____

_____

Good morning Holy Spirit, will you speak to me today.

Devotional: Power in Weakness

2 Corinthians 12:9 (KJV)

"And he said unto me, My grace is sufficient for thee: for my strength is made perfect in weakness. Most gladly therefore will I rather glory in my infirmities, that the power of Christ may rest upon me."

1. God's Grace Is on You

No matter what you're facing, God's grace is at work in your life. It's not only His unmerited favor but also the divine enablement to face challenges and fulfill His purpose. Instead of trying to earn or deserve His grace, recognize it as a free gift He lavishes upon you daily.

2. God's Grace Works for You

Grace isn't passive; it actively operates on your behalf. Whether you're struggling with temptation, enduring a trial, or feeling overwhelmed by life's demands, His grace empowers you to keep moving forward. God's strength fills in where your own efforts fall short, ensuring you have what you need right when you need it.

3. Weakness Invites God's Power

The apostle Paul learned that his greatest breakthroughs happened in moments of weakness. Why? Because those moments create space for God's power to shine. When you admit your limitations and rely on Him, you open the door for Christ's strength to manifest. Embrace your weaknesses as opportunities for God to display His might.

Prayer

Lord, thank You for Your sufficient grace that meets me exactly where I am. Help me to lean on You in my moments of weakness rather than striving in my own strength. May Your power rest upon me and be glorified in every trial I face. In Jesus' name, Amen.

Reflection Question

In what area of your life do you need to acknowledge your weakness today, allowing God's grace and power to work more fully on your behalf?

Action Question:

How can I serve God today?

_____

_____

_____

_____

Good morning Holy Spirit, will you speak to me today.

Devotional: The God Who Answers

Matthew 7:7–8 (KJV)

"Ask, and it shall be given you; seek, and ye shall find; knock, and it shall be opened unto you: For every one that asketh receiveth; and he that seeketh findeth; and to him that knocketh it shall be opened."

1. He's a God of Desire

God not only hears our requests; He cares about the desires of our hearts. When we ask, we're acknowledging our dependence on Him for provision and guidance. Bringing your petitions to God isn't a sign of weakness; it's an act of faith, trusting that He delights in fulfilling righteous desires.

2. He's a God of Expectation

Jesus' instruction to "seek" implies active pursuit. Searching out God's will and wisdom shows we believe He has the answers we need. Expectation is the posture of faith—confidently awaiting God's response. When we diligently seek Him, we position ourselves to receive His direction and revelation.

3. He's a God of Open Doors

Knocking at God's door signifies persistence and hope for an invitation into something new. He promises that when we knock, it shall be opened. In Christ, no barrier is too strong to withstand His sovereign power. Whether you're praying for an opportunity, a breakthrough, or a miracle, keep knocking. He opens doors in His perfect timing and way.

Prayer

Lord, thank You for being a God who invites us to ask,
seek, and knock. Increase my faith to trust that You
desire good things for me, that my expectations are safe
in Your hands, and that You will open every door
according to Your will. In Jesus' name, Amen.

Reflection Question

Which door in your life do you need to knock on today,
trusting God to open it at just the right time?

Action Question:

How can I serve God today?

_____

_____

_____

_____

Good morning Holy Spirit, will you speak to me today.

Devotional: Strength in Weakness

2 Corinthians 12:10 (KJV)

"Therefore I take pleasure in infirmities, in reproaches, in necessities, in persecutions, in distresses for Christ's sake: for when I am weak, then am I strong."

1. Failure Is Eminent

Life brings moments of weakness and perceived failures—whether it's a shortcoming, a setback, or a time when you simply don't measure up to your own expectations. The Apostle Paul acknowledged these "infirmities," recognizing they're part of our human condition. Expecting the possibility of failure helps us stay humble and aware of our constant need for God's grace.

2. Failure Is Not Final

Paul found reason to "take pleasure" in his weaknesses because he knew they weren't the end of his story. In Christ, weakness doesn't spell defeat; it sets the stage for God's power to work. The moment you recognize your inability to handle a situation is the moment you're most open to God's intervention. Failure, in God's hands, can become a stepping stone rather than a stumbling block.

3. Every Failure Is a Lesson

"For when I am weak, then am I strong." It's in your weakest moments that God's strength shines brightest. Every failure, shortfall, or disappointment can teach you more about His sufficiency. Rather than succumbing to defeat, see each "infirmity" as an invitation to deeper reliance on Christ. His power is perfected in your inability, transforming failures into lessons of His faithfulness.

Prayer

Lord, thank You for Your power that's made perfect in my weakness. Help me to see failures not as the end, but as opportunities for You to show Your strength in my life. Teach me to learn from every shortfall and to rely on Your grace day by day. In Jesus' name, Amen.

Reflection Question

Where in your life do you need to shift your perspective on failure, allowing God's strength to shine through your weakness?

Action Question:

How can I serve God today?

_____

_____

_____

_____

Good morning Holy Spirit,will you speak to me today.

Devotional: The Marks of a Blessed Life

Isaiah 32:8 (KJV)

"But the liberal deviseth liberal things; and by liberal things shall he stand."

1. It Shows on Your Life

A "liberal" person in Scripture refers to one who is generous and open-handed. Generosity naturally flows from a heart blessed by God. This trait begins to show in your decisions, priorities, and interactions. A truly blessed life radiates kindness and compassion—others can see God's abundance reflected in the way you live.

2. It's Evident in the People Around You

When you're generous, those around you benefit. Whether it's sharing resources, offering time, or extending grace, your liberality touches others, uplifting and encouraging them. A hallmark of a blessed life is the impact you have on family, friends, and even strangers who experience God's blessing through your willingness to give.

3. It Becomes the Signature of Your Life

Over time, generosity becomes a defining characteristic—your spiritual signature. When you consistently devise "liberal things," you build a legacy of giving and goodness that stands the test of time. Generosity isn't just an occasional act; it's a lifestyle rooted in your relationship with the One who generously provides for you.

Prayer

Lord, thank You for showing me that a blessed life is one
marked by generosity. Teach me to be open-handed and
kind, reflecting Your goodness to everyone around me.
Help me live in a way that my generosity becomes a
lasting testimony to Your abundant grace. In Jesus'
name, Amen.

Reflection Question

How can you practice generosity—whether in resources,
time, or attitude—so that it becomes a defining signature
of your life?

Action Question:

How can I serve God today?

_____

_____

_____

_____

Good morning Holy Spirit, will you speak to me today.

Devotional: The Compassionate Healer

Matthew 14:14 (KJV)

"And Jesus went forth, and saw a great multitude, and was moved with compassion toward them, and he healed their sick."

1. He Sees You

Before Jesus performed any miracle, He saw the multitude. He notices every person's need, including yours. You are not overlooked or forgotten. He's aware of your struggles, hurts, and desires. His compassionate gaze isn't just for biblical crowds—it's for you, right where you are.

2. His Love Won't Fail You

Compassion is more than pity; it's love in action. Jesus didn't merely acknowledge the crowd's need; He was moved to respond. That same unwavering love extends to you today. Whatever you face, His love remains steady, relentless, and willing to step in on your behalf.

3. He's Healing You

Jesus didn't stop with comforting words—He healed their sick. In your life, He offers healing for body, mind, and spirit. Sometimes it's physical restoration; other times, it's a mended heart, renewed hope, or freedom from anxiety. Trust that He is working to bring wholeness, even if you don't see the full picture yet.

Prayer

Lord, thank You for seeing me with eyes of compassion
and for loving me without fail. Strengthen my faith to
trust in Your healing touch, whether I need physical,
emotional, or spiritual restoration. Remind me daily that
You are near, caring for my every need. In Jesus' name,
Amen.

Reflection Question

Where in your life do you need to embrace Jesus'
compassionate love and healing touch today, trusting that
He sees you and cares for your needs?

Action Question:

How can I serve God today?

_____

_____

_____

_____

Good morning Holy Spirit, will you speak to me today.

Devotional: The Shield and the Lifter

Psalm 3:3 (KJV)

"But thou, O LORD, art a shield for me; my glory, and the lifter up of mine head."

1. God Is Our Protector

In a world that often feels dangerous and uncertain, God stands as a steadfast shield around His people. This isn't just a metaphor for physical protection—it includes spiritual and emotional guarding as well. When we trust Him, no threat or trial can overtake us without His knowledge and permission. Rest in the assurance that He's watching over you, ready to defend you from every angle.

2. God Is a God of Dignity and Honor

David calls the Lord his glory, reminding us that real honor and worth come from God alone. When circumstances try to rob you of your dignity, remember that your value is secured by the One who created you. He crowns you with His love and favor, restoring what life's hardships may have tried to take away. You don't have to strive for validation from the world; God has already affirmed your worth in Him.

3. God Will Encourage You Through It All

He's not only your protector and your glory—He's also the One who lifts your head. When burdens weigh you down, He gently raises your chin, reminding you to keep your eyes on Him. His constant encouragement and presence are sufficient to carry you through every challenge. Let Him strengthen your heart and boost your spirit, no matter what you're facing.

Prayer

Lord, thank You for being my shield, my source of honor, and the One who lifts my head. In times of trouble or discouragement, help me to remember that You watch over me, affirm my worth, and encourage me every step of the way. Teach me to trust You more deeply and to rest in Your faithful care. In Jesus' name, Amen.

Reflection Question

In what specific situation do you need to experience God's protective shield, His affirming grace, or His uplifting encouragement today? How can you invite Him into that circumstance right now?

Action Question:

How can I serve God today?

_____

_____

_____

_____

Good morning Holy Spirit, will you speak to me today.

Devotional: Strength in Weakness

Psalm 73:26 (KJV)

"My flesh and my heart faileth: but God is the strength of my heart, and my portion forever."

1. Can't Depend on My Heart

Our emotions can fluctuate, and our physical strength has limits. When we rely solely on ourselves—our feelings, willpower, and abilities—we eventually hit a wall. Recognizing our own fragility reminds us we need a power greater than our own to carry us through life's challenges.

2. God Will Always Come Through

Though our human capacity fails, God's capacity never does. He's not limited by our weaknesses or circumstances. He remains steadfast, ready to support, renew, and sustain us when we can't go on. Knowing God is our portion gives us hope and comfort, even in our darkest moments.

3. I'll Trust Him Every Time

Because God doesn't fail, we can place our full trust in Him. Whenever life's trials threaten to overwhelm us, we can recall the truth that He is our strength. Instead of giving in to anxiety or despair, let faith rise as you lean on the One who promises never to forsake you.

Prayer

Lord, thank You for being the strength of my heart when
I'm weak and the portion I can depend on forever.
Remind me to place my trust in You rather than in my
own limited abilities. Help me face each challenge with
confidence in Your unwavering support. In Jesus' name,
Amen.

Reflection Question

In what area of your life do you most need to depend on
God's strength rather than your own today, and how can
you actively surrender that to Him?

Action Question:

How can I serve God today?

_____

_____

_____

_____

Good morning Holy Spirit, will you speak to me today.

Devotional: No Fear in the Valley

Psalm 23:4 (KJV)

"Yea, though I walk through the valley of the shadow of death, I will fear no evil: for thou art with me; thy rod and thy staff they comfort me."

1. Life Won't Escape Moments of Fear

Every life journey encounters dark valleys—moments when danger, uncertainty, or anxiety seem overwhelming. Accepting that fear is part of our human experience helps us prepare our hearts to rely on God when trouble arises.

2. Hard Times Don't Always Indicate the Wrong Path

Just because your path is difficult doesn't mean you've strayed. Sometimes the valley is part of God's plan to grow your faith and deepen your trust in Him. Instead of doubting your journey, lean into His guiding presence.

3. Fear Has an Immediate Opponent

Your fear isn't left unchecked; it meets a direct challenge: "I will fear no evil." That decision arises because God is by your side. Whenever fear knocks, remember it immediately faces the One who is greater than any threat or trial.

4. God Promises Protection

God's rod and staff are symbols of His protection and guidance. The rod wards off predators; the staff directs and reassures. Together, they illustrate that He is both your defender and your shepherd, committed to keeping you safe and leading you forward.

Prayer

Lord, thank You for walking with me through every valley I face. Help me to remember that moments of fear are normal, but I can stand firm knowing You are my protector and guide. Strengthen my faith so that in every season, I trust Your presence and find comfort in Your rod and staff. In Jesus' name, Amen.

Reflection Question

Which "valley" are you currently walking through, and how can you lean on God's promised protection and guidance to conquer fear in this season?

Action Question:

How can I serve God today?

_____

_____

_____

_____

Good morning Holy Spirit, will you speak to me today.

Devotional: Victory, Confidence, and Overflow

Psalm 23:5 (KJV)

"Thou preparest a table before me in the presence of mine enemies: thou anointest my head with oil; my cup runneth over."

1. God Is My Victory

When David speaks of a table prepared in the presence of his enemies, it's a profound image of God's triumph on our behalf. Even when opposition surrounds you, the Lord sets the stage for your victory. You don't have to fight for a seat at the table; God already reserves one for you. His presence ensures that no foe can rob you of the peace He's established.

2. God Is My Confidence

Being anointed with oil symbolizes favor, blessing, and the touch of God's Spirit. This divine anointing instills holy confidence that goes beyond human courage. It reminds you that you're chosen, set apart, and equipped for the purpose He's called you to. When God anoints you, you can stand tall, knowing that His approval outweighs any doubt or criticism you might face.

3. God Is My Overflow

David's cup runs over, pointing to the lavish abundance God pours into our lives. He doesn't ration His blessings; He gives them generously. When you walk under His guidance, you don't just survive—you flourish. The overflow isn't just for you to keep; it's also for sharing with others as a testimony of God's extravagant love and provision.

Prayer

Lord, thank You for preparing a table before me even in challenging circumstances. Remind me that my victory is secure in You, my confidence is found in Your anointing, and my life can overflow with Your goodness. Teach me to walk in faith and gratitude, sharing Your abundance with the world. In Jesus' name, Amen.

Reflection Question

Where do you most need to experience God's victory, confidence, or overflow in your life right now, and how can you open yourself to receiving it?

Action Question:

How can I serve God today?

_____

_____

_____

_____

Good morning Holy Spirit, will you speak to me today.

Devotional: A Promise of Goodness and Mercy

Psalm 23:6 (KJV)

"Surely goodness and mercy shall follow me all the days of my life: and I will dwell in the house of the LORD for ever."

1. God Is My Assurance

This verse begins with the word "surely," a word of confident expectation. It's a declaration that God's goodness and mercy are not mere possibilities but guaranteed realities in the believer's life. You can rest assured that His presence, favor, and loving kindness will accompany you, no matter the circumstances.

2. God is the Pursuing Shepherd

The original language suggests that goodness and mercy pursue or chase after us. Our Shepherd doesn't wait passively; He actively follows us with blessings. Even when we stray or face hardships, God's love and grace remain unrelenting, determined to bring us back into His protective care.

3. God Is My Hiding Place

The promise culminates in the assurance of dwelling in God's house forever. This isn't just about a physical location—it's about abiding in His presence. His house is a refuge, a place where we find security, rest, and intimate fellowship with Him. No matter what challenges you encounter, you have a divine hiding place in the Lord's unfailing care.

Prayer

Lord, thank You for the certainty of Your goodness and mercy following me every day. I praise You for actively pursuing me with Your love and for being my safe refuge. Teach me to live confidently in Your assurance, knowing that I can always dwell in Your presence. In Jesus' name, Amen.

Reflection Question

In what way can you more fully embrace God's "pursuit" of goodness and mercy in your life, allowing Him to be your hiding place in every circumstance?

Action Question:

How can I serve God today?

_____

_____

_____

_____

Good morning Holy Spirit, will you speak to me today.

Devotional: Shine in the Darkness

John 1:5 (KJV)

"And the light shineth in darkness; and the darkness comprehended it not."

1. You Are the Light

As a follower of Christ, His Spirit resides in you, making you a bearer of His light. You don't generate the light on your own; rather, you reflect Jesus' nature. When you walk in His truth and love, you illuminate the spaces you enter, revealing hope where despair once lingered.

2. Darkness Can't Handle You

Darkness cannot extinguish God's light; it can neither overwhelm nor comprehend it. The same is true for you. Because of Christ in you, the darkness around you must retreat. You stand victorious, not by your own power, but by the unstoppable light of Christ shining through you.

3. To Shine Is What You Do

You were created to radiate God's love and truth. Sharing His hope and peace is not just an option—it's part of your spiritual DNA. As you live out the gospel in word and deed, your light continues to pierce the darkness, drawing others to the One who is the source of all light.

Prayer

Lord, thank You for making me a vessel of Your light. Strengthen me to shine brightly in places that need hope, reminding me that darkness has no power over me. Help me walk in love and truth so that others see Your light through my life. In Jesus' name, Amen.

Reflection Question

In what specific area of your life can you shine Christ's light more boldly this week, trusting that the darkness cannot overcome it?

Action Question:

How can I serve God today?

_____

_____

_____

_____

Good morning Holy Spirit, will you speak to me today.

Devotional: Peace in Every Way

2 Thessalonians 3:16 (KJV)

"Now the Lord of peace himself give you peace always by all means. The Lord be with you all."

1. Recognize the Origin of Peace

True peace doesn't come from a change in circumstances; it comes from the Lord Himself. He is the source of peace. When life feels chaotic or unpredictable, remember that genuine peace is found in turning your heart toward the One who rules over every storm.

2. Know That He's All-Time Peace

God's peace isn't momentary; it's constant. "Always by all means" reminds us He's not limited by time or situations. Whether you're soaring through blessings or trudging through challenges, He can sustain you with an inner calm that transcends your immediate reality.

3. Know That He's Peace in Every Way

The Lord offers peace that touches every part of your life—spiritual, emotional, relational. It's complete, covering all the ways you might feel unsettled. In Jesus, you find peace for today's trials, assurance for tomorrow's uncertainties, and hope for eternity.

Prayer

Lord, thank You for being the source of lasting peace. Teach me to turn to You in every season, trusting in Your constant and complete peace. Fill my heart with calm assurance, reminding me that You are with me through every challenge and victory. In Jesus' name, Amen.

Reflection Question

Which specific area of your life needs God's peace today, and how can you trust Him to be your constant source of calm in that situation?

Action Question:

How can I serve God today?

_____

_____

_____

_____

Good morning Holy Spirit, will you speak to me today.

Devotional: The Reign of Peace

Colossians 3:15 (KJV)

"And let the peace of God rule in your hearts, to which also ye are called in one body; and be ye thankful."

1. Give Yourself Permission to Be at Peace

Life's demands often make it feel like peace is a luxury instead of a right. Yet God's Word encourages us to let His peace rule—implying that we need to allow or permit peace to take hold. You don't have to feel guilty for resting or choosing calm. Take a moment to release anxieties and invite God's calming presence into your heart.

2. Allow God's Peace to Have Ruling Authority in Your Life

We can be quick to let worries, fears, or stress dictate our actions, but Paul instructs us to let God's peace make the final call. Imagine it as an umpire making decisions in your life—when doubts arise, let peace override them; when conflicts flare, let peace set the direction. Submitting to His peace ensures your decisions align with His gentle wisdom.

3. Always Give Thanks

Paul closes this verse by calling us to thankfulness. Gratitude anchors us in God's goodness and helps us maintain perspective. When we recognize even the smallest blessings, we create an environment where peace naturally thrives. Make thankfulness a habit—your

heart and mind will find rest in remembering how
faithful God has been.

Prayer

Lord, thank You for offering me Your peace, which
surpasses all human understanding. Teach me to give
myself permission to rest in You, to allow Your peace to
rule my heart, and to remain thankful in every situation.
May my life reflect the calm assurance that comes from
trusting You completely. In Jesus' name, Amen.

Reflection Question

Where in your life do you need to let God's peace overrule
worry or stress, and how can gratitude help you maintain
that posture of calm assurance?

Action Question:

How can I serve God today?

_____

_____

_____

_____

Good morning Holy Spirit, will you speak to me today.

Devotional: The Power of Persistent Prayer

James 5:18 (KJV)

"And he prayed again, and the heaven gave rain, and the earth brought forth her fruit."

1. Prayer Changes Things

When Elijah prayed, heaven responded and rain fell, ending the drought. Prayer isn't just a spiritual exercise—it's a dynamic interaction with the living God. Through prayer, circumstances can shift, hearts can soften, and miracles can unfold.

2. Faith Prays Again

Elijah didn't stop praying after a single request; he prayed again. True faith isn't discouraged by initial silence or delay. It presses in, believing that God is more than able to answer. Persistence in prayer demonstrates trust in His perfect timing and provision.

3. Prayer and Faith Move the Hand of God

While God is sovereign, He invites us to partner with Him through prayer. When our petitions align with His will, our faith-filled prayers can spark divine intervention. We don't coerce God, but our persistent cries reflect our confidence that He actively works on our behalf.

4. God's Hand Brings the Victory

Ultimately, it's God's hand that makes the difference. As you persevere in prayer, remember that the final outcome is in His control. Whether it's rain in a drought or breakthrough in a trial, the victory belongs to the Lord, who never fails to provide for His people.

Prayer

Lord, thank You for inviting me to pray and for hearing my requests. Strengthen my faith so I won't give up, even when answers seem delayed. I trust that prayer, combined with faith, moves Your mighty hand. May Your will be done in my life, bringing victory that reveals Your glory. In Jesus' name, Amen.

Reflection Question

What situation in your life needs persistent prayer and faith today, trusting that God's hand will ultimately bring victory?

Action Question:

How can I serve God today?

_____

_____

_____

_____

Good morning Holy Spirit, will you speak to me today.

Devotional: The Key to Prosperity

Deuteronomy 29:9 (KJV)

"Keep therefore the words of this covenant, and do them, that ye may prosper in all that ye do."

1. Know the Word, Know Him

God's Word is more than just commandments; it's His covenant—a reflection of His character and His love for us. To truly know Him, you must spend time in His Word. As you study Scripture, you deepen your relationship with God, understanding His heart and His plans for your life.

2. Know the Word, Obey Him

Knowing God's Word isn't enough; obedience is the next step. His instructions are designed to guide you toward a life of blessing and purpose. When you align your actions with His Word, you demonstrate your trust in Him and position yourself to receive His promises.

3. Know Him, Obey Him, Prosper

True prosperity comes from a life rooted in God. It's not just material wealth but spiritual richness, peace, and fulfillment in every area of life. When you know God, obey His Word, and trust His guidance, you'll see His hand moving in ways that bring lasting success and purpose.

Prayer

Lord, thank You for Your covenant and the guidance found in Your Word. Help me to know You more through Scripture and to walk in obedience to Your commands. Teach me to trust Your ways so I may prosper in all that I do, bringing glory to Your name. In Jesus' name, Amen.

Reflection Question

How can you deepen your knowledge of God's Word and apply it in obedience to see His prosperity in your life?

Action Question:

How can I serve God today?

_____

_____

_____

_____

Good morning Holy Spirit, will you speak to me today.

Devotional: Hold On to Your Confidence

Hebrews 10:35 (KJV)

"Cast not away therefore your confidence, which hath great recompence of reward."

1. Don't Let Life Shut Your Mouth

Life's circumstances can sometimes feel overwhelming, tempting you to silence your faith. Hardships, disappointments, and setbacks might make you question if speaking God's promises aloud is worthwhile. But Scripture encourages us not to throw away our bold confidence in what He has declared. Even in the midst of trials, keep your voice of faith alive.

2. Speak What You Believe

Your words hold power—when you declare God's truth, you align your heart and mind with His will. Speaking promises out loud isn't just wishful thinking; it's a proclamation of trust. When you verbally affirm who God is and what He's promised, you build an atmosphere of hope and expectation around your life.

3. Believe What You Speak

It's one thing to say something; it's another to truly believe it. Faith rooted in God's Word transforms mere words into life-changing declarations. Ask God to deepen your conviction so your confessions aren't empty phrases but heartfelt affirmations of truth. When belief matches your speech, you open the door to see God move mightily on your behalf.

4. Confidence Brings Reward

God promises a "great recompense of reward" for those who hold fast to their confidence in Him. This isn't just about material gain—it includes peace, strength, and testimony of God's faithfulness. By refusing to let go of your bold trust, you position yourself to receive the blessings He's eager to pour out.

Prayer

Lord, thank You for reminding me not to let life's challenges silence my faith. Help me to speak Your promises with conviction and to truly believe every word I confess. Strengthen my confidence in You, and let it bring forth the rewards You've promised. In Jesus' name, Amen.

Reflection Question

What specific promise or truth from God's Word do you need to keep speaking and believing in your current circumstances, trusting Him for the reward He has promised?

Action Question:

How can I serve God today?

_____

_____

_____

_____

Good morning Holy Spirit, will you speak to me today.

Devotional: Unwavering Faith

Hebrews 10:23 (KJV)

"Let us hold fast the profession of our faith without wavering; (for he is faithful that promised;)"

1. Keep Your Head

When doubts or distractions come, it's easy to lose focus and let fear cloud your judgment. Holding fast to your faith means keeping a clear mind and remembering God's promises. Stay centered on His truth rather than the chaos around you. Keeping your head allows you to see life's storms for what they are—temporary moments that God will navigate you through.

2. Keep the Faith

Faith isn't just a concept; it's your lifeline to God's character and promises. To "hold fast" is to cling to it with every fiber of your being, refusing to let go even when circumstances suggest otherwise. Faith grows when tested. As you persevere, you discover that it's not your strength but God's faithfulness that sustains you.

3. He'll Keep His Promise

The reason you can remain steady is because "He is faithful that promised." God's track record is perfect—He never fails to keep His word. Whatever He has spoken over your life, trust Him to bring it to completion. You don't have to waver because your foundation rests on the One who never breaks a promise.

Prayer

Lord, thank You for being the faithful God who keeps every promise. Help me to keep my head clear, my faith strong, and my eyes fixed on You. Remind me daily that I can hold fast to my faith because You are the One who never fails. In Jesus' name, Amen.

Reflection Question

Which promise of God do you need to cling to today, trusting His unwavering faithfulness to bring it to pass?

Action Question:

How can I serve God today?

_____

_____

_____

_____

Good morning Holy Spirit, will you speak to me today.

Devotional: Established and Protected

2 Thessalonians 3:3 (KJV)

"But the Lord is faithful, who shall establish you, and keep you from evil." 1. God Won't Fail You

When we consider God's faithfulness, we're reminded that He has never broken a promise. In a world where people and circumstances can let us down, God stands as the unshakable rock we can rely on. His faithfulness is a sure foundation, guaranteeing He won't fail or forsake you.

2. God Will Plant You

To "establish" means to set firmly in place. God isn't interested in leaving you in a state of uncertainty or instability. As you trust Him, He roots you deeper in His Word and strengthens you for whatever comes your way. The trials you face can't uproot you when God Himself is the One who's planting you.

3. God Will Shield You

This verse assures us that God will keep us from evil. He doesn't merely watch from a distance—He actively protects and guards your heart, mind, and spirit. No matter what the enemy may attempt, God's faithful hand remains over your life, shielding you from harm

Reflection Question

Where do you need God's faithfulness to establish and protect you most right now, and how can you trust Him more in that specific area?

Action Question:

How can I serve God today?

_____

_____

_____

_____

Good morning Holy Spirit, will you speak to me today.

Devotional: Glory After This

Romans 8:18 (KJV)

"For I reckon that the sufferings of this present time are not worthy to be compared with the glory which shall be revealed in us."

1. This Is Just the Path

The challenges and hardships we face are part of the journey, but they are not the destination. Every difficulty molds and shapes us for the greater purpose God has in store. Remember, the path may be hard, but it is leading somewhere glorious. Trust the process and keep moving forward.

2. Trouble Won't Last Always

Your current trials are temporary. They may feel overwhelming now, but they have an expiration date. God promises that His joy and peace will outlast any suffering you experience. Let this assurance sustain you when the weight of the moment feels unbearable—better days are ahead.

3. There Will Be Glory After This

God is preparing something extraordinary for you. The glory He will reveal in and through you is far greater than anything you're enduring. This isn't just about heavenly rewards; it's about the transformative work He's doing in your life now. Your pain will not be wasted—it will lead to His glory being revealed.

Prayer

Lord, thank You for reminding me that my current struggles are temporary and that Your glory will shine through in the end. Help me to trust You through the process and hold on to the hope that greater things are ahead. Strengthen my faith as I wait for the glory that will come after this. In Jesus' name, Amen.

Reflection Question

How can you stay focused on God's promise of future glory while enduring the challenges of the present?

Action Question:

How can I serve God today?

_____

_____

_____

_____

Good morning Holy Spirit, will you speak to me today.

Devotional: Victory Through God

Psalm 60:12 (KJV)

"Through God we shall do valiantly: for he it is that shall tread down our enemies." 1. Only Through God

True victory doesn't come from our own strength or strategies but through God's power. When we rely on Him, we're tapping into a source of strength that is far greater than anything we possess. He is the reason for our confidence and the foundation of every triumph we achieve.

2. You Have the Courage to Win

Because God is with you, you can face any battle with boldness. His presence in your life equips you with the courage to overcome obstacles that once seemed impossible. Remember, you're not fighting alone—God's power is working through you, giving you the ability to act valiantly.

3. He's Got Your Light Work

The verse assures us that God will tread down our enemies. This means He takes on the heavy lifting in our battles. Whether it's a spiritual, emotional, or physical challenge, you can trust that He's handling what you cannot. Your role is to trust Him, step forward in faith, and watch Him handle the rest.

Prayer

Lord, thank You for being the source of my strength and the One who fights my battles. Help me to trust You fully and act boldly, knowing that through You, I can do valiantly. Teach me to rest in the assurance that You're handling what's beyond my control. In Jesus' name, Amen.

Reflection Question

What battle are you facing today, and how can you trust God to give you the courage to win and handle what feels impossible?

Action Question:

How can I serve God today?

_____

_____

_____

_____

Good morning Holy Spirit, will you speak to me today.

Devotional: A Reason to Praise the Lord

Psalm 117:1-2 (KJV)

"O praise the LORD, all ye nations: praise him, all ye people. For his merciful kindness is great toward us: and the truth of the LORD endureth for ever. Praise ye the LORD."

1. His Loving Kindness

God's merciful kindness is unmatched. His love is not only abundant but also intentional, tailored to meet your every need. This is a love that covers your mistakes, strengthens you in weakness, and never gives up on you. If you're searching for a reason to praise the Lord, look no further than His unfailing love that is poured out daily.

2. His Enduring Truth

In a world where truth can feel fleeting and unreliable, God's truth stands forever. His promises, principles, and plans are unwavering. They were true yesterday, they are true today, and they will remain true forever. Praising God for His enduring truth is a way of affirming that His Word is a firm foundation in every season of life.

3. It's All for You

What makes God's loving kindness and enduring truth even more amazing is that they're directed toward you. His care isn't generic; it's personal. He extends His mercy and truth specifically to His people, ensuring you are never overlooked or forgotten. This reality makes your praise personal, as you thank Him for how He moves uniquely in your life.

Prayer

Lord, I praise You for Your merciful kindness and enduring truth. Thank You for loving me in ways that are beyond my understanding and for being the steady foundation in my life. Teach me to live in gratitude and to proclaim Your goodness to others. In Jesus' name, Amen.

Reflection Question

How can you make today a day of intentional praise, reflecting on God's loving kindness and His truth that never fails?

Action Question:

How can I serve God today?

_____

_____

_____

_____

Good morning Holy Spirit, will you speak to me today.

Devotional: The Reward of the Pursuit

Proverbs 21:21 (KJV)

"He that followeth after righteousness and mercy findeth life, righteousness, and honour."

1. It's the Pursuit

Life is about what we intentionally chase after. When your focus is on righteousness and mercy, you align your path with God's will. This pursuit shapes your character and decisions, leading to blessings that only God can provide. It's not about arriving at perfection but about persistently following His ways.

2. Pursue What's Right

Righteousness means living in a way that reflects God's standards and His truth. It requires courage to stand for what is right, even when it's inconvenient or unpopular. Each step toward righteousness strengthens your relationship with God and points others to His goodness.

3. Pursue Kindness

Mercy and kindness are reflections of God's heart. As you actively show compassion to others, you create an atmosphere where His love is evident. Pursuing mercy means choosing grace over judgment, forgiveness over resentment, and generosity over selfishness.

4. God Answers with Honor

God promises rewards for those who seek righteousness and mercy—life, righteousness, and honor. These aren't just worldly accolades but eternal blessings that reflect His favor. When you follow His ways, God elevates you in His time, granting you the honor that comes from walking closely with Him.

Prayer

Lord, thank You for the promise that pursuing righteousness and mercy leads to life and honor. Help me to focus on what's right and to show kindness to others, reflecting Your character in all I do. Strengthen my heart to stay committed to this pursuit, trusting in Your rewards. In Jesus' name, Amen.

Reflection Question

What specific area of your life can you align more with righteousness and mercy today, and how can you trust God to honor your pursuit?

Action Question:

How can I serve God today?

_____

_____

_____

_____

Good morning Holy Spirit, will you speak to me today.

Devotional: Trust That Lasts Forever

Psalm 125:1-2 (KJV)

"They that trust in the LORD shall be as mount Zion, which cannot be removed, but abideth for ever. As the mountains are round about Jerusalem, so the LORD is round about his people from henceforth even for ever."

1. Trusting God Gives Strength

When you place your trust in God, you're grounded in His unshakable power. Like Mount Zion, you become immovable, able to stand firm no matter what life throws at you. Trusting Him strengthens your faith and equips you to endure challenges with courage and resilience.

2. Trusting God Gives Stability

Mount Zion symbolizes permanence, a stability that nothing can disrupt. Trusting God anchors you in His promises, providing a solid foundation that life's uncertainties cannot erode. While the world shifts and changes, God remains constant, and so does your footing when you rely on Him.

3. Trusting God Assures Your Protection

The imagery of mountains surrounding Jerusalem reminds us of God's unwavering protection. He surrounds His people, guarding and shielding them from harm. Trusting in the Lord means you're never exposed or vulnerable—His presence is always with you, offering eternal security.

Prayer

Lord, thank You for being my strength, stability, and protector. Help me to trust You fully, knowing that You are unchanging and always present. Teach me to stand firm in faith, resting in the assurance that You surround me with Your love and care. In Jesus' name, Amen.

Reflection Question

How can you deepen your trust in God today, allowing Him to strengthen, stabilize, and protect you in the challenges you face?

Action Question:

How can I serve God today?

_____

_____

_____

_____

Good morning Holy Spirit, will you speak to me today.

Devotional: Hope in the Unseen

Romans 8:25 (KJV)

"But if we hope for that we see not, then do we with patience wait for it."

1. Believe for It

Hope begins with belief. Even when the outcome is unseen, your faith allows you to trust in God's promises. Believing doesn't mean ignoring the reality of your circumstances; it means anchoring yourself in the truth that God is able to do exceedingly more than you can imagine.

2. Expect It

Hope isn't passive—it's an active expectation. When you hope for what you cannot see, you position your heart to receive what God has promised. Expectation fuels your faith and keeps you moving forward, even when the journey feels long or uncertain.

3. Wait for It

Patience is the companion of hope. Waiting isn't easy, but it's where growth happens. In the waiting, God refines your character, strengthens your faith, and aligns your heart with His will. Trust that His timing is perfect, and the unseen blessing will come at the right moment.

Prayer

Lord, thank You for giving me hope, even in the unseen. Help me to believe in Your promises, expect Your goodness, and patiently wait for Your perfect timing. Teach me to trust that what I cannot see now is already being prepared for me in Your plan. In Jesus' name, Amen.

Reflection Question

What are you hoping and waiting for today, and how can you actively trust God during the waiting season?

Action Question:

How can I serve God today?

_____

_____

_____

_____

Good morning Holy Spirit, will you speak to me today.

Devotional: Trust the Process

Philippians 1:6 (KJV)

"Being confident of this very thing, that he which hath begun a good work in you will perform it until the day of Jesus Christ."

1. He Started It

God initiated the good work in you. From the moment you accepted Christ, He began shaping and molding your life for His glory. You didn't stumble into His grace by accident—it was His divine plan all along. Trust that the work He started is intentional and filled with purpose.

2. He's Working It

The process of growth can be challenging, but God is actively working in your life. Even when you don't see it, He's aligning circumstances, refining your character, and drawing you closer to Him. His work is continuous, ensuring that you are being transformed day by day.

3. He'll Finish It

God doesn't leave things unfinished. His promise is that the good work He started in you will be completed. No setback, failure, or delay can stop Him. When you feel discouraged, remember that He is the Author and Finisher of your faith, and He will carry you to completion.

Prayer

Lord, thank You for starting a good work in me and for faithfully continuing it. Help me to trust Your process, even when I don't understand it. Remind me that You are the One who will finish what You began in my life. Strengthen my confidence in Your faithfulness. In Jesus' name, Amen.

Reflection Question

In what area of your life do you need to trust that God is still working and will bring His good work to completion?

Action Question:

How can I serve God today?

_____

_____

_____

_____

Good morning Holy Spirit, will you speak to me today.

Devotional: The Power of an Open Mouth

Psalm 8:2 (KJV)

"Out of the mouth of babes and sucklings hast thou ordained strength because of thine enemies, that thou mightest still the enemy and the avenger."

1. Open Your Mouth with Praise

God has ordained strength through praise, even from the mouths of the smallest and most vulnerable. When you open your mouth to glorify God, you silence the enemy's lies. Praise shifts your focus from your struggles to God's greatness, reminding you that His power is far greater than any challenge you face.

2. Open Your Mouth with Purpose

Your words carry weight, and when spoken with purpose, they align with God's will. Speak life, declare His promises, and proclaim His truth. Purposeful words are a weapon against the enemy, dismantling strongholds and building faith in your own heart and in those around you.

3. Open Your Mouth with Power

The words you speak have the power to overcome the enemy. Through Christ, even the weakest among us can defeat darkness with faith-filled declarations. Use your voice as a tool to call on God's power, stilling the enemy and advancing His kingdom.

Prayer

Lord, thank You for the strength You have placed in my words. Teach me to open my mouth with praise, purpose, and power. Help me to use my voice to glorify You and to silence every lie of the enemy. May my words always reflect Your truth and bring honor to Your name. In Jesus' name, Amen.

Reflection Question

How can you use your words today to praise God, declare His promises, and silence the enemy's lies in your life?

Action Question:

How can I serve God today?

_____

_____

_____

_____

Good morning Holy Spirit, will you speak to me today.

Devotional: Trusting God's Promises

2 Corinthians 1:20 (KJV)

"For all the promises of God in him are yea, and in him Amen, unto the glory of God by us."

1. God Made You a Promise

God's Word is filled with promises that cover every aspect of life—provision, protection, healing, peace, and salvation. These promises are not generic; they are personal. He made them for you, knowing your needs and desires. Take hold of His promises with confidence, knowing they are spoken over your life.

2. God Keeps His Promises

God is not like man; He doesn't break His word. Every promise He makes is a guarantee, sealed in Christ. His faithfulness ensures that what He has spoken will come to pass. Even if the fulfillment seems delayed, you can trust that He is working behind the scenes to bring His promises to fruition.

3. His Promises Bring Him Glory

When God fulfills His promises, it's not just for your benefit—it's for His glory. Each answered prayer, breakthrough, and blessing becomes a testament to His power and faithfulness. Your life becomes a reflection of His greatness, pointing others to the God who always keeps His word.

Prayer

Lord, thank You for the promises You have made to me.
Help me to trust in Your faithfulness and to stand firm in
the assurance that You always keep Your word. Let my
life reflect Your glory as I walk in the fulfillment of Your
promises. In Jesus' name, Amen.

Reflection Question

What promise from God are you holding onto today, and
how can you trust Him to fulfill it in His perfect timing?

Action Question:

How can I serve God today?

_____

_____

_____

_____

Good morning Holy Spirit, will you speak to me today.

Devotional: Strength for the Fight

Psalm 144:1 (KJV)

"Blessed be the LORD my strength, which teacheth my hands to war, and my fingers to fight."

1. God Will Give You Strength to Fight

God doesn't send you into battles unprepared. He is your source of strength, equipping you to face every challenge. When you feel weak or overwhelmed, lean into His power. His strength is made perfect in your weakness, ensuring you can stand firm in every spiritual or physical fight.

2. God Will Teach You How to Fight

God not only empowers you but also equips you with the wisdom and skills to fight effectively. He teaches your hands and fingers—symbolizing your efforts and strategies—to navigate life's battles with precision. Trust His guidance as He shows you when to act, when to wait, and how to overcome.

3. God Will Give You Victory in the Fight

The ultimate promise is victory. God doesn't just leave you in the fight; He ensures that you emerge victorious. Whether your battle is against fear, temptation, or circumstances, trust that He has already secured the outcome. His faithfulness guarantees that you will triumph in His name.

Prayer

Lord, thank You for being my strength and for teaching me how to fight the battles I face. Help me to trust Your guidance and rely on Your power. I praise You for the victories You've already secured for me. In Jesus' name, Amen.

Reflection Question

What battle are you facing today, and how can you trust God to strengthen, teach, and lead you to victory?

Action Question:

How can I serve God today?

_____

_____

_____

_____

Good morning Holy Spirit, will you speak to me today.

Devotional: God, Our Keeper and Shield

Psalm 121:5-6 (KJV)

"The LORD is thy keeper: the LORD is thy shade upon thy right hand. The sun shall not smite thee by day, nor the moon by night."

1. Our God Is a Keeper

God watches over you with tender care and unwavering faithfulness. He is your Keeper, ensuring that no harm comes to you outside of His perfect will. His eyes are always on you, guiding your steps and protecting you from seen and unseen dangers. Trust that He never slumbers or forgets His promise to keep you.

2. Our God Is a Shield

God is your shade and shield, providing constant protection. Whether you're facing physical threats, emotional burdens, or spiritual attacks, He stands as your defense. His covering ensures you're never exposed to more than you can bear. He guards you, even in the smallest details of life.

3. Our God Will Cover

From the scorching heat of the day to the hidden dangers of the night, God's presence surrounds you. His covering is complete, offering peace and safety in every season and circumstance. No matter what you face, His divine protection ensures that you remain under His care.

Prayer

Lord, thank You for being my Keeper, my Shield, and my constant Covering. Help me to trust in Your protection, knowing that You are always watching over me. Strengthen my faith as I rest in Your care, and remind me daily of Your unfailing love. In Jesus' name, Amen.

Reflection Question

How can you rely more fully on God's keeping and shielding presence in the challenges you're facing today?

Action Question:

How can I serve God today?

_____

_____

_____

_____

Good morning Holy Spirit, will you speak to me today.

Devotional: Joy in the Harvest

Psalm 126:5 (KJV)

"They that sow in tears shall reap in joy."

1. Sowing Is Essential

Every harvest begins with a seed. In life, sowing represents the effort, sacrifice, and faith we invest in pursuing God's purpose. Whether you're sowing into relationships, ministry, or personal growth, your faithfulness in planting seeds will set the stage for God's blessings. Without sowing, there can be no reaping.

2. Sowing Is Not Always Convenient

Sowing in tears reminds us that life's hardest seasons often require the greatest acts of faith. Planting seeds while enduring trials, pain, or uncertainty can feel overwhelming, but God sees your labor and your tears. Your faithfulness during difficult times is an act of worship, and it will not go unnoticed by Him.

3. Sowing Always Brings a Harvest

God promises that those who sow in tears will reap in joy. Your labor is not in vain, and the seeds you plant in faith will produce a harvest of blessings. The joy that comes from God's provision and faithfulness will far outweigh the pain of the sowing season.

Prayer

Lord, thank You for the promise that every seed I sow in faith will bring a harvest of joy. Help me to remain faithful in planting, even when it's hard or inconvenient. Strengthen my trust in Your timing and remind me that You are the God of the harvest. In Jesus' name, Amen.

Reflection Question

What seeds of faith or effort are you planting today, and how can you trust God to bring a harvest of joy in His perfect timing?

Action Question:

How can I serve God today?

_____

_____

_____

_____

Good morning Holy Spirit, will you speak to me today.

Devotional: Go Win

2 Timothy 4:7 (KJV)

"I have fought a good fight, I have finished my course, I have kept the faith."

1. Fight the Fight

Life is full of spiritual battles, but the good news is that you're not fighting alone. God equips you with His Word, His Spirit, and His strength to stand firm against every challenge. The fight of faith isn't about perfection; it's about perseverance. Keep fighting, knowing that victory is already yours in Christ.

2. Run the Race

Your journey is unique—God has given you a specific course to run. Stay focused on the path He has set before you, and don't be distracted by what others arc doing. Run with endurance, keeping your eyes on the ultimate prize: finishing well and hearing, "Well done, good and faithful servant."

3. Keep the Faith

In the face of trials, doubts, or discouragement, hold tightly to your faith. Trust in God's promises, even when the race feels long or the fight seems tough. Faith is your anchor, keeping you grounded in hope and ensuring you finish strong.

Prayer

Lord, thank You for giving me the strength to fight, the endurance to run, and the faith to persevere. Help me to stay focused on the course You've set for me and to fight with confidence, knowing You are with me. Strengthen my faith so I can finish well for Your glory. In Jesus' name, Amen.

Reflection Question

What area of your life requires you to fight, run, or hold onto faith today, and how can you rely on God to help you finish well?

Action Question:

How can I serve God today?

_____

_____

_____

_____

Good morning Holy Spirit, will you speak to me today.

Devotional: Do it Jesus Way

Matthew 11:29 (KJV)

"Take my yoke upon you, and learn of me; for I am meek and lowly in heart: and ye shall find rest unto your souls."

1. Walk in Meekness

Jesus invites us to take His yoke—a symbol of partnership and shared burden. Meekness isn't weakness; it's strength under control. Walking in meekness means surrendering to God's guidance and trusting His ways over your own. As you learn from Him, you discover a life marked by grace and gentleness.

2. Walk in Humility

Humility is the foundation of discipleship. Jesus, the ultimate example of humility, calls us to lay down pride and self-reliance, choosing instead to trust in His leadership. When you walk in humility, you open your heart to His teachings and allow Him to shape your life according to His purpose.

3. You Then Find Peace

Rest comes when you align your life with Christ. By learning from Him and walking in His ways, you release the weight of trying to do it all on your own. His yoke is easy, and His burden is light, leading to a peace that surpasses all understanding. True rest is found in surrendering to His love and guidance.